Norwich and the Norfolk Broads

AA Publishing

Produced by AA Publishing

© The Automobile Association 1997
Maps © The Automobile Association 1997

First published 1997

All rights reserved. No part of this publication may be reproduced,
stored in a retrieval system, or transmitted in any form or by any
means – electronic, photocopying, recording or otherwise – unless
the written permission of the publisher has been obtained before-
hand.

Published by AA Publishing (a trading name of Automobile
Association Developments Limited, whose registered office is
Norfolk House, Priestley Road, Basingstoke, Hampshire RG24
9NY; registered number 1878835).

ISBN 0 7495 1495 7

A CIP catalogue record for this book is available from the British
Library.

The contents of this book are believed correct at the time of printing.
Nevertheless, the publishers cannot be held responsible for any
errors or omissions or to changes in the details given in this book
or for the consequences of any reliance on the information provided
by the same. Material in this book has been previously published
by AA Publishing in various publications.

AA Publishing would like to thank Roland Smith, Head of
Information Services for The Peak National Park, and Chairman of
The Outdoor Writers' Guild for his knowledge and assistance.

Colour separation by BTB, Digital Imaging, Whitchurch, Hampshire

Printed and bound by George Over Ltd, Rugby

NORFOLK

Flatness, enormous panoramic skies and cloudscapes, windmills and turkeys are all associated with Norfolk, a county whose distinctive identity has been supported by its relative isolation from the rest of the country and the fact that it is as close to Amsterdam as it is to its own capital, London.

Cold-shouldered by the Industrial Revolution, it is mainly prosperous and efficient arable farming country, with few towns of any size. In areas the soil is dry and sandy, but elsewhere there is some of the wettest and richest land in England. In the northwest the fens spill over from Cambridgeshire, and the delightful old town of King's Lynn is an island port on the Great Ouse, close to the Wash. Northeast from here are the royal estate of Sandringham and the scented lavender fields at Heacham. Norfolk's great naval hero, Lord Nelson, came from Burnham Thorpe, where his father was rector.

Norfolk's reputation for flatness is somewhat exaggerated. Apart from the Fens and the marshes, much of the county is a gently rolling landscape. A chain of nature reserves stretches along the low-lying North Norfolk coast with its small harbours, saltmarshes and mudflats carpeted in sea lavender, where diminutive rivers wriggle their way to the North Sea through channels and creeks, attracting walkers, small-boat sailors, cockles and whelks, and multitudes of birds.

This part of Norfolk that juts out into the North Sea accounts for the presence of the many birds that may be seen here, as they fly down Britain's coastline in autumn or fly directly across the sea from Scandinavia.

The shrine to the Virgin Mary at Walsingham draws many pilgrims, while Cromer is a pleasant seaside resort with a famous lifeboat. Further on down the coast are sand and shingle beaches and a constant battle against the encroaching sea. People digging for peat inland in medieval times unintentionally created the Broads, northeast of Norwich, which provide some 200 miles (320km) of inland waterways for cruising and sailing.

Norwich itself, the county town, is a lively and enjoyable market, financial, cultural and university centre, with a beautiful cathedral of Caen stone, brought from Normandy by water, and one of the best museums in the country in an odd-looking Norman castle. Great Yarmouth, a popular resort on the coast, was a redoubtable herring port until overfishing put paid to the industry after World War II.

Thetford has an abundance of Georgian and medieval houses in its pretty centre. The town is the capital of the Breckland of southwestern Norfolk, stretching across the border into Suffolk, an area of sandy heaths, marshes and diminutive lakes, which was covered with conifers by the Forestry Commission in the period between the two world wars. The forest supports a unique wildlife including roe deer, fallow deer, muntjac and a few remaining red squirrels.

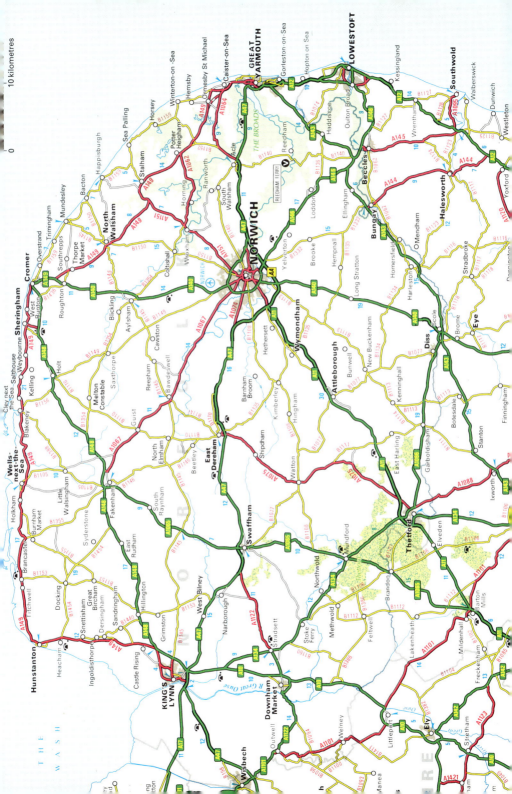

ACLE–BINHAM

ACLE
SMALL TOWN ON A47, 8 MILES (13KM) W OF GREAT YARMOUTH

The pleasant village of Acle stands in some of Norfolk's most beautiful and important wetland countryside. Acle was granted a market charter in the 13th century, and market day is still an important event in the area. The Church of St Edmund King and Martyr is more than 900 years old, and has an interesting round tower.

ATTLEBOROUGH
SMALL TOWN OFF A11, 5 MILES (8KM) SW OF WYMONDHAM

This busy market town dating from Saxon times has a Norman church. Some townspeople sailed with the Pilgrim Fathers to America.

AYLSHAM
SMALL TOWN ON B1354, 12 MILES (19KM) N OF NORWICH

A market town that grew to prosperity under the ownership of John of Gaunt, son of Edward III.
(See also Cycle ride: Blicking Hall and the Marriot Way, page 7.)

BACONSTHORPE CASTLE
BACONSTHORPE, VILLAGE OFF A148, 3 MILES (5KM) SE OF HOLT

The romantic ruins of the castle dominate the small village. This was really a moated and semi-fortified house, built by the Heydon family in the 15th century. The gatehouses, curtain walls and towers remain.
Open all year, daily.

BANHAM ZOO
BANHAM, VILLAGE ON B1113, 6 MILES (10KM) NW OF DISS
THE GROVE. TEL: 01953 887771

Enjoy a day out among some of the world's rare and endangered animals including snow leopards, cheetahs, Grevy's Zebra, jackass, penguins, many exotic birds and primates. Daily animal feeding sessions and keeper talks are not only fun but educational too. Wander through the deer park, woodland walk, and monkey jungle island. Other attractions include an adventure playground.
Open all year, daily. Closed 25–26 Dec.

BINHAM
VILLAGE ON B1388, 5 MILES (8KM) SE OF WELLS-NEXT-THE-SEA

The ruins of the Benedictine priory, founded in 1100 on the outskirts of this village, are situated in open arable farmland. The Norman nave serves as the church of St Mary and the Holy Cross. Inside, there is a seven-sacrament font and, on a side altar table, there is the Tobruk Cross, which was shaped from shell cases to commemorate those who died in North Africa in World War II.
The glory of the priory is its west front, built before 1244 from honey-coloured Barnack stone and local flint.

The beautiful setting for the parish church at Binham – almost all that remains now of the 11th-century Benedictine priory

BLICKLING HALL

Cycle ride

A fairly level and easy-going ride, this route begins at the fine National Trust property of Blickling Hall, and incorporates a variety of parkland tracks, peaceful country lanes and a section of well surfaced disused railway track, The Marriott Way. Diversions along the route include a rose garden, a timeless estate village and fascinating churches.

INFORMATION

Total Distance
21 miles (33.5km), with 6 miles (9.5km) off-road

Difficulty
Moderate

OS Map
Landranger 1:50,000 sheet 133 (North East Norfolk)

Tourist Information
Aylsham (summer only), tel: 01263 733903; Norwich, tel: 01603 666071

Cycle Hire
Reepham Station Museum of Shops (summer), tel: 01603 871187

Nearest Railway Station
Aylsham. Bure Valley Railway links with main line at Hoveton and Wroxham for Norwich

Refreshments
Pub and good tea room with family facilities at Blickling Hall; Mill Restaurant at Itteringham and Rose Tea Room at Mannington Hall Gardens; pubs at Heydon, Reepham and Aylsham (also cafés). Excellent picnic spots in Blickling Park

Cyclists on the Marriott Way

BLICKLING HALL AND THE MARRIOTT WAY

7

Cycle ride

BLICKLING HALL AND THE MARRIOTT WAY

BLICKLING HALL

START
The ride starts from the National Trust car park (free) at Blickling Hall, which is located on the B1354, 1½ miles (2.5km) north-west of Aylsham and 15 miles (24km) north of Norwich.

DIRECTIONS
1. From the car park follow the path to the information board and sign stating 'Park Only'. Turn left along the estate road, bearing right at a fork by some cottages to enter Blickling Park. After a short distance take the waymarked bridleway diagonally left across the park (Weavers' Way). Proceed for 1 mile (1.5km), passing a track to the

An unusual sculpture of horseshoes at Heydon Park

Mausoleum, and keeping to the left of Great Wood to reach a parking area and lane.

2. Turn left, then bear right at the next junction along the Bure Valley to a further junction by the Walpole Arms and the Mill Restaurant. Keep right, cross the river and pass through Itteringham, following signs to Mannington. After ½ mile (1km) turn left towards Corpusty and shortly pass Mannington Hall on your right and the entrance to the gardens. Continue, and at a T-junction turn left along a gently undulating lane. Stay on this for 1½ miles (2.5km) to the junction of the B1354 and B1149.

3. Continue straight on into Saxthorpe. Cross the River Bure

and turn right in front of the shop, signed 'Little London'. Almost immediately turn left by The Dukes Head pub to climb out of the village. The views are good; stay on this lane for 1½ miles (2.5km), passing Cropton Hall, to reach a T-junction. Turn left, then at a crossroads bear left again into the attractive and unspoilt estate village of Heydon.

4. Return to the crossroads and proceed straight over, signposted to Salle. In about a mile keep right at a junction around Salle Park, then take the next lane right towards Salle church. Continue through the hamlet, turn left at a T-junction towards Reepham, and proceed for 1 mile (1.5km) to the B1145 on the edge of the village.

BLICKLING HALL

Cycle ride

5. Keep straight ahead towards Reepham, then in a few yards turn left, opposite the old railway bridge, and pass through a gate to join the Marriott Way – a good, surfaced trail along the former railway track. In 2 miles (3km) pass under a bridge and fork left to climb on to an embankment (the former platform of Cawston Station). Continue to a level crossing and cross a by-road.

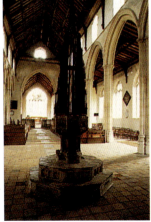

6. Proceed for a further 4 miles (6.5km) through open country to the end of the trail, at a gate adjoining the B1354 in Aylsham. Turn left through the town centre, remaining on the B-road and in $^1/_2$ mile (1km) fork left on an unclassified lane. In 1 mile (1.5km) at Abel Heath (NT), fork right and pass through the hamlet of Silvergate to reach the B1354,

The lofty interior of Salle church

Blickling Hall gardens in summer

BLICKLING HALL AND THE MARRIOTT WAY

Cycle ride

BLICKLING HALL

Looking across to Salle church

PLACES OF INTEREST

Blickling Hall
Flanked by 17ft (5m) dark yew hedges planted in the 17th century, this magnificent Jacobean brick-fronted hall is one of the great houses of East Anglia. Dutch gabling, mullioned windows and domed turrets characterise the exterior. Inside there are fine collections of furniture, pictures and tapestries, and a spectacular Jacobean plaster ceiling in the 123ft (37.5m) Long Gallery (moulded in the 1620s) is very impressive. The gardens are also worth exploring. Open Apr–Oct, most days. Tel: 01263 733084

Mannington Hall Gardens
Outstanding gardens surround a moated medieval manor house (not open). There is a scented garden, and a rose collection. The gardens are open on selected summer days, the park all year round.
(See also page 59).

Heydon
This is a most attractive village, built around a charming green where time seems to have stood still, at the end of a dead-end lane. Heydon Hall (open by appointment only) dates from 1581 and has an E-shaped front. (See also page 46.)

Salle church
The tiny village of Salle is the unlikely setting for a 15th-century cathedral-like church full of rich treasures, apparently totally out of proportion to the tiny parish it serves. It was built by three wealthy families: the Briggs, the Fontaynes and the Boleyns. Of particular note is the unusual font.

Aylsham
An old market town on the River Bure, Aylsham has many attractive Georgian houses. The famous landscape gardener Humphry Repton (1752–1818) is buried in the churchyard, with the epitaph he composed himself.

WHAT TO LOOK OUT FOR

Both the churches at Heydon and Salle hide notable features. Remarkable 14th-century wall paintings, first disclosed in 1970, grace the walls in Heydon church, and the splendid painted rood screen dates from 1480. Well worth finding in Salle church are the 26 carved oak stalls. Some have good carvings of human heads, others boast birds and animals; note the swan, squirrel, dragon and ape. Look out, too, for the strange horse sculptures created from horseshoes in Heydon.

BRESSINGHAM

The church in this village was rebuilt in 1527, and has bench ends carved into fanciful shapes, including inter-twining foliage. This is a suitable theme for these parts, as the grounds of the hall nearby have been transformed into 6 acres (2.5ha) of internationally famous gardens.

Alan Bloom is an internationally recognised nurseryman and a steam enthusiast, and has combined his interests to great effect at Bressingham. There are three steam-hauled trains: a 10.25in gauge garden railway, a 15in gauge running through $2^{1}/_{2}$ miles (4km) of the wooded Waveney Valley, a 2ft gauge running through $2^{1}/_{4}$ miles (3.5km) of Europe's largest hardy plant nursery and a standard gauge engine giving demonstrations on certain days. The Dell Garden has 5,000 species of perennials and alpines, grouped in island beds; Foggy Bottom has wide vistas, pathways, trees, shrubs, conifers and winter colour (restricted opening). There is a collection of 50 road and rail engines, a number restored to working order. A steam roundabout is another attraction and the Norfolk fire museum is housed here. Various events are held here during the year.

Open – Steam Museum and Dell Garden: Apr–Sep, daily.

BRESSINGHAM
VILLAGE ON A1066, 3 MILES (5KM) W OF DISS

Bressingham Steam Museum and Gardens
TEL: 01379 687386 & 687382

Alan Bloom's Heather and Conifer Garden at Bressingham

THE BROADS

The Broads is the newest member of the National Park family, and it has the youngest landscape. But if anyone had suggested some 40 years ago, when the first National Park was being designated, that this enchanted area of mysterious, misty fens and slow, winding waterways was anything other than natural, no-one would have believed them. However, we now know that this entire network of dykes and broads on the borders of Suffolk and Norfolk is entirely man-made – and it is none the less beautiful for that. The area was given long overdue protection when it was created a National Park in all but name in 1989.

The Broads is a mecca for lovers of tranquillity. Head of Information Services for The Peak National Park, and Chairman of The Outdoor Writers' Guild, Roland Smith, describes his experience of The Broads:
'The cormorants sat motionless on the windmill, silhouetted like two metal weather-vanes, one on the topmost edge of the sail and the other perched on the tail vane. There was no danger that their belvedere would be disturbed, for the weather on that winter's day in the heart of the Broads was misty and eerily calm. The black shapes of the cormorants seemed to remain in position for most of the seminar which I was attending at the How Hill environmental centre for the Broads, adding to the impression of their permanence.

The view from the Sun Room at How Hill was both a constant distraction and an inspiration during the long meetings, for, from its lofty heights – lofty, that is, for the low-lying Broads – the vista extended over the winding River Ant, the waving, tawny reedmarshes of Reedham, Clayrack and Bisley, and down to the red-brick towermill at Turf Fen. It was this glorious panorama which attracted Edward Boardman, the Norwich architect, and inspired him to build the charming Edwardian, reed-thatched and gabled house of How Hill as the family home.

How Hill itself is a prominent knoll of sand and gravel laid down in the outwash from a melting ice sheet during the Ice Ages. Once part of a much

THE BROADS

The white-sailed Boardman's Windmill on the River Ant near How Hill

Gazetteer

THE BROADS

Hickling Broad, one of the quieter backwaters

larger plateau, it was reduced to its present size by the abrasive action of the same glacial meltwaters which signalled the end of the Ice Age. At a mere 40ft (12m) above the sea, How Hill is still the highest point of the Broads National Park.

First recorded as 'Haugr', or 'Haugh Hill', meaning high point, it owes its name to the Viking invaders from Denmark who first nosed the inquisitive prows of their proud longships into the shallow staithe below the hill on the River Ant during the 9th century. The word staithe is found regularly along the east coast of England between Northumberland and Norfolk, and is pure Danish, meaning a quay, or landing point for ships. The view from How Hill was beautifully described by Walter White in a guidebook to Eastern England first published in 1865:

"…. a big knoll, thickly covered with oat-grass, from the top of which we had a pleasant view, and enjoyed the scent of elder blossom with which *we had become familiar; broad reedy flats, pastures of various colour, coarse swamps, bright patches of poppies, irregular patches of water, windmills and dykes, and the narrow stream repeating its lazy curves across the vast level."*

He was describing a typical Broads landscape as it was before the invasion of tourism that began with the arrival of the railway in the 1870s. But those marshy levels which ring How Hill remain some of the finest reedmarshes in Britain, and the home of rare, water-loving wildlife. Inhabitants include the mercurial hen harrier, which can often be seen quartering the reed-beds on floating, buoyant wings; the elusive bittern, whose booming notes echo across the marshes in the spring; the handsome bearded tit or reedling, and the more dowdy reed warbler, which builds its neat, circular nest using living reedstems as supports.

The huge wintering flocks of teal, wigeon, coot and redshank were the Norfolk wildfowlers' stock-in-trade in days gone by, and the spectacular swallowtail butterfly, Britain's biggest, still beats its showy way across the fen in high summer, attracting lepidopterists from all over the country.
It is the only British member of the *papilionidae* family, more usually found in the tropics, and makes a magnificent sight as it feeds on the flowers of campion and milk parsley.

On the way to How Hill staithe, it is worth inspecting the charming little former eel-catchers' cottage of Toad Hole. This reed-thatched, red-brick two-up, two-down cottage, hidden away in the willows, has been faithfully reconstructed and furnished in traditional style by the National Park authority, and one half expects to see Ratty and Mole appearing round the corner.

Moored up at the staithe can sometimes be found traditional Norfolk wherry sail boats. These broad-beamed, black-sailed wherries were the main form of cargo transport on the Broads for 200 years. One called *Hathor*, built at

THE BROADS

nearby Reedham in 1905, plies a charter trade for tourists along with a handful of other such craft.

It took the combined research skills of a geographer, a botanist and a geomorphologist to finally crack the code which explained the creation of the Broads. Until then, less than 40 years ago, the enchanted, wet wilderness of the Broads had been regarded as an entirely natural landscape.

In fact, the 117 square miles (303 sq km) of the Norfolk Broads National Park, centered around three major rivers, the Bure, the Yare and the Waveney, and their tributaries, the Ant, the Thurne and the Chet, which all meander down to the sea at Great Yarmouth, have been said to represent the greatest human modifications ever made to the natural landscape of this country. Geomorphologists had noted from borings that the original sides of the water-filled basins of the Broads were almost vertical and cut directly through the natural peat of the valley floors. Also, some Broads contained narrow, parallel peninsulas of peat, and islands whose sides were also

A busy stretch at Horning

steeply sloping or vertical. All this pointed to the fact that they were man-made; but where was the historical evidence? The answer to that question came from historians carefully sifting through the records of St Benet's Abbey, on the banks of the River Bure at Holme. The lonely, romantic ruins of this Benedictine monastery (a favourite subject for Victorian artists) are dominated by the 18th-century, round, red-brick towermill built inside the gatehouse. St Benet's, one of the most important historic sites in the Broads, probably dates from the 9th century, but was rebuilt and endowed with three manors by King Canute in AD 1020.

The records showed that from the 12th century onwards certain areas in Hoveton parish were set aside for peat-digging, and in one year alone no fewer than a million turves were cut. This large-scale extraction, mainly for fuel, went on continuously for over two centuries, and by the early 14th century the cathedral priory at nearby Norwich alone was using nearly 400,000 turves annually from the area we now know as the Broads.

The total area excavated by those medieval peat-diggers has been estimated at about 2,600 acres (1,052ha), and the transformation of the 12ft (4m) deep peat-diggings to Broads resulted from gradual flooding from the 13th century onwards. At about this time there was a very slight change in the relative levels of the land and sea, and coastal and low-lying areas became increasingly at risk from flooding. Although there were some attempts to dredge peat underwater, using a special rake known as a dydle, by the 15th century working had become so difficult that peat-cutting was no longer profitable and had been abandoned.

Since then, the shallow lakes have gradually been infilled with dead vegetation and sediment. Tithe maps of the 1840s show an area of nearly 3,000 acres (1,214ha) of open water, whereas today's figure is more like half that total. Until recently, the waters of the Broads supported a wide variety of water plants which form the basis of the aquatic food chain and in turn support a great variety of insects, small animals and fish. But by the 1950s a significant change had begun to occur, and the waterways became increasingly choked by a luxuriant growth of underwater plants and algae.

THE BROADS

The reason for this change was that there had been an enormous increase in the nutrient levels of the water, due to effluent from sewage treatment works and the run-off from the increased application of fertiliser on adjacent farmland. The result was that the formerly crystal-clear waters of the Broads were turned into a murky peasoup by the floating algae – a process known to scientists as eutrophication.

The Broads authority has taken steps to halt this process by pumping out the enriched mud from the bottom of some Broads by suction dredging. The results, in places like Cockshoot Dyke and Cockshoot Broad, have been encouraging, with a dramatic improvement in the water quality and the re-establishment of submerged water plants such as waterlily, hornwort and bladderwort.

The 125 miles (200km) of lock-free navigable rivers and Broads in the National Park make it one of the most intensively used inland waterways in Europe, and it is estimated that there were more than 2,000 hire cruisers on the Broads in the mid-1970s. Some 200,000 holidaymakers now use weekly-let motor cruisers annually, and this is also a cause for concern to the Broads authority as the wash from motorised pleasure craft can break up the reed mats on the banks of the Broads, and eventually the banks themselves can be washed away. Artificial bank protection, the imposition of speed limits on boating, the isolation of certain stretches of bank, and research into hull design are among the solutions currently being investigated.

In total, the Broads National Park receives over three million annual visitors, most of whom come to enjoy the unspoiled beauty of Broads, dykes and fens, the wet, tangled alder carr woodlands, and the wide expanses of grazing marshes under those vast East Anglian skies. Halvergate Marshes, just to the west of Great Yarmouth and bordering Breydon Water, could

THE BROADS

be said to be the birthplace of the Broads National Park, for in 1985 it became the site of the experiment which was to result in the first Environmentally Sensitive Area (ESA) in England. Here, farmers are paid to manage the extensive windmill-dotted marshes by traditional grazing methods, and this should conserve their unique features for posterity.

When the idea of National Parks in Britain was being discussed in the 1940s, the eminent biologist Julian Huxley wrote from Paris saying that he could not imagine a group of British National Parks being set up which did not include the Broads. It took 40 years to happen, but now the Broads – that 'last enchanted land' – is an integral, important and very special member of Britain's National Park family'.

Boats on the River Thurne

Gazetteer

BRUNDALL—BURE VALLEY RAILWAY

BRUNDALL
Village off A47, 6 miles (10km) E of Norwich

The long straggling village of Brundall is situated on high ground overlooking the River Yare, and has developed into an important Broads boating centre. The Yare at this point flows through attractive woodland before passing an extensive marina.

BURE VALLEY RAILWAY
Tel: 01263 733858
Wroxham, 7 miles (11km) NE of Norwich

When the writer and broadcaster Miles Kington opened the Bure Valley Railway in 1990, it marked the completion of the longest miniature railway to be built in Britain since the 1920s. The 9-mile (14.5-km) line links the 'capital' of the Norfolk Broads at Wroxham with the town of Aylsham, where the market square is ringed with fine 18th-century houses, and it serves a local transport function as well as being a tourist attraction. Conveniently, the British Rail and Bure Valley stations at Wroxham are connected by a footbridge, and the town centre at Aylsham is only a short walk from the station.

The 15-in gauge railway is built on the trackbed of a Great Eastern Railway branch line that left the Norwich to Cromer line at Aylsham and meandered through gently rolling country to join the Dereham-Wells line at the isolated junction of County School. Although the line was open for freight until the early 1980s, 17 bridges had to be repaired, a $1/4$-mile (0.5-km) tunnel built under the Aylsham bypass and 6,000 tons of crushed shingle brought in to replace the ballast.

The journey in the comfortable carriages takes visitors past the walls of the Elizabethan Little Hautbois Hall, its blocked-up windows still recalling the aesthetic damage done by the window tax, which was in force from 1695 to 1851. Heading to Aylsham, the train soon runs parallel to the River Bure, where swans can sometimes be seen in majestic flight and geese are ten a penny. The village of Buxton with Lammas, the two separated by the Bure, is served by a station on the line and is an interesting place to break the journey. This was the

BURE VALLEY RAILWAY

gazetteer

birthplace of Thomas Cubitt, the entrepeneur who built more of 19th-century London than anyone else. The attractive Church of St Andrew can be glimpsed from the train, but the Quaker Burial Ground and resting place of the author of *Black Beauty*, Anna Sewell, has to be sought out.

After rattling through the tunnel into Aylsham station, the train draws to a halt under a huge overall roof, a very grand terminus for a railway of this small gauge. The engine shed beside the station gives visitors the opportunity to admire the fine collection of surprisingly powerful locomotives, the most recent additions being based on an Indian Railways' narrow gauge design. Keen walkers can use their legs in either direction, since the line runs alongside the Bure Valley Walk; this path connects with a network of paths from Norwich to North Walsham created by Broadland District Council. Guides to the routes are available.

Train service: Etr–Sep, most days.

The Bure Valley Railway runs over the old Great Eastern Wroxham-Aylsham line

Gazetteer

BURGH CASTLE-BURNHAM THORPE

BURGH CASTLE
VILLAGE OFF A143, 3 MILES (5KM) SW OF GREAT YARMOUTH

A marina, with all available boating facilities, is the first place where boats can moor when making their way upstream on the River Waveney from Great Yarmouth.

The Castle

Burgh Castle was built in the 3rd century AD by the Romans, as one of a chain of forts along the Saxon Shore – the coast where Saxon invaders landed. Originally on an estuary, it is now several miles from the sea on flat marshland. Sections of the massive walls still stand (some parts faced with flint), and are protected by bastions where 'ballistae' or giant catapults may have been mounted.
Open any reasonable time.

Berney Arms Windmill
TEL: 01493 700605

Access is by boat from Great Yarmouth or by rail to Berney Arms station: the road to the mill is unsuitable for cars. This lonely, seven-storey landmark dates back to the 19th century, and helped to drain the marshes. In earlier years it was also used to grind clinker for cement. The machinery for both functions can be seen.
Open Apr–Sep, daily.

BURNHAM MARKET
VILLAGE OFF A149, 5 MILES (8KM) W OF WELLS-NEXT-THE-SEA

The Burnhams form a group of seven villages spread along the Burn Valley. Burnham Market encompasses Burnhams Westgate, Sutton and Ulph. It has a spacious village green fringed with some elegant 18th-century houses. The main crop of the 19th century in nearby farms was barley, and several maltings have been converted into houses.
(See also Cycle ride: Holkham Park and the Burnhams, page 49.)

BURNHAM NORTON
HAMLET ON A149, 1 MILE (2KM) N OF BURNHAM MARKET

Burnham Norton is an unspoiled hamlet standing at the edge of the reclaimed saltmarshes. A painted wine-glass pulpit is in the church.

BURNHAM OVERY
HAMLET ON B1155, 1 MILE (2KM) NE OF BURNHAM MARKET

Burnham Overy was once a port, but as the sea began to recede, Overy Staithe was built. Burnham Overy is a charming village with a watermill and windmill standing side by side. Across lavender-covered saltmarshes stands Overy Staithe with a fine range of granaries and maltings owned by the National Trust.

BURNHAM THORPE
VILLAGE OFF B1155, 2 MILES (3KM) SE OF BURNHAM MARKET

The Lord Nelson inn reveals that Burnham Thorpe was the birthplace of Lord Admiral Horatio Nelson. The 13th-century church bears tribute to him with a bust above his father's tomb and flags from battleships. Nelson's actual house no longer exists, but the village is a pleasant place to visit with a wide green and Georgian buildings.
(See also Cycle ride: Holkham Park and the Burnhams, page 49.)

BURNHAM THORPE

This pleasant walk follows in the footsteps of the young Horatio Nelson, who was born in the village, through pastures and along tracks down to the salt marshes and creeks of the North Norfolk coast.

Grid ref: TG852418
INFORMATION
The walk is about 4 miles (6.5km) long.
Level easy ground.
About ½ mile of road walking.
A few stiles to cross.
Dogs should be kept on leads on the road; under control everywhere else.

Pub in Burnham Overy Staithe with bar meals and garden.
Ice cream van often on staithe in summer.
The sea wall at Burnham Overy Staithe is suitable for picnics.

Low tide at Burnham Overy Staithe – a peaceful scene

DIRECTIONS
From the main gate of the church, walk away from the church across the grass and on to a track. Bear right and almost immediately take the signposted footpath on the left, crossing over a stile and keeping a hedge on the right. Go through a gateway into a large meadow with a number of ponds. Keep the hedge on the right until reaching a grove of trees, then bear left keeping trees to the right. As the trees come to an end bear right to a footpath sign and stile. Cross the stile, climb the bank of a disused railway, then go left and after 100yds (91.5m) turn right down the bank. Follow the path up a gentle hill with a hedge on the right, cross into the next field and continue in the same

Walk

BURNHAM THORPE

direction until reaching a road by a cottage. Turn right and after about 200yds (183m), where the houses end, turn left down a track.

Keep straight on. Eventually sea, dunes and salt marsh come into view. Continue until the track becomes metalled and the outskirts of Burnham Overy Staithe are reached. At the main road cross over by The Hero pub and follow the narrow lane (East Harbour Way) down to the staithe. (A path to the right runs along the sea wall to the beach at Gun Hill.) Follow the road around to the left. The road then turns inland back to the main road. Here turn right, walking along the footpath by the main road until the coast path is signed; this runs parallel with the road but just within the field.

Shortly before the tall black windmill turn left, crossing the road and proceeding up a wide track. Eventually reach a minor road and turn right. Follow this road until it bends to the right, just before Burnham Overy Town church. Go straight ahead through the churchyard, then turn left along the road for about ¼ of a mile (0.5km). Turn right by the cottage and telephone box and retrace your steps to the start point.

Burnham Thorpe church

Horatio Nelson's father was rector here from 1755–1802 and the great naval hero was born in Burnham Thorpe in 1758. The rectory where he was raised was later demolished. The church has a small exhibition on Nelson's life, including a cross made of timbers from HMS *Victory*, and the ship's flags. There is also the font in which he was christened.
(See also page 22).

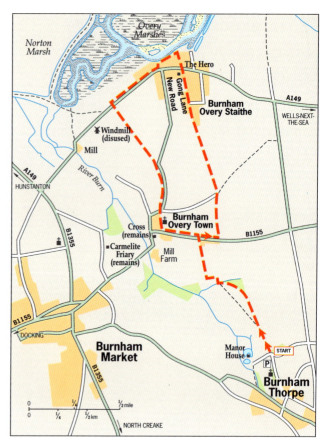

WHAT TO LOOK OUT FOR

The meadows near Burnham Thorpe church can be good for wild duck, especially in winter. Many common butterflies are found along the hedgerows during summer. In winter look out for brent geese, especially on the coastal sections. Both churches on the walk are worth a visit.

CAISTER-ON-SEA – CASTLE RISING

Caister has a long and fascinating history. It was settled by the Romans, and remains of their camp, including the south gateway, a town wall built of flint with brick bonding courses, and part of what may have been a seamen's hostel, can still be visited. In 1432, the powerful Fastolf family built Caister Castle, one of the first brick buildings in England. In 1904, a tragic lifeboat disaster robbed Caister women of husbands, sons and brothers.

The rugged outlines of sturdy Roman walls with the little Saxon church huddled against them are evocative of the history of this ancient village. It is thought that Queen Boudicca (Boadicea) had her headquarters here, or near by, when she fought against the Romans. It is possible that a Roman capital was built here to quell further uprisings by the Iceni.
  Boudicca was a 1st-century queen of the Iceni tribe of East Anglia. Boudicca was beaten and her two daughters raped in AD 61 by the Romans who were plundering her people. She raised the Iceni in furious revolt and they sacked Colchester and London before being routed by Roman troops. Boudicca died soon afterwards – possibly committing suicide. Tradition has her buried in London, on Parliament Hill or beneath platform ten at King's Cross railway station. She became a folk heroine as a symbol of resistance to oppression, and a 19th-century statue of her in her war chariot stands proudly by Westminster Bridge in London.

The village is dominated by one of the most splendid Norman keeps in England. Castle Rising also has a row of red-brick almshouses built in 1807, and a 15th-century cross.

1327 the unfortunate King Edward II was horribly murdered in Berkeley Castle on the orders of his wife, Queen Isabella, and her lover, Roger Mortimer. At this time, Edward's heir, Edward III, was only 15 years old, and Mortimer and Isabella were able to rule England together by manipulating the young King. This state of affairs continued for three years until Edward III began to take matters back into his own hands. Learning of the roles of his mother and Mortimer in the death of his father, Edward had Mortimer tried for treason and hanged in 1330. Isabella, as guilty as Mortimer, was spared trial and execution, but was banished from court. She spent the last 30 years of her life at Castle Rising, joining an order of nuns called the Poor Clares. Although it is easy to look at the strong walls of the mighty keep at Castle Rising and imagine the fallen Isabella confined, lonely and forgotten in her castle prison, there is no evidence that she was physically constrained there. In fact, there is some suggestion that she

CAISTER-ON-SEA
SMALL TOWN OFF A149, 3 MILES (5KM) N OF GREAT YARMOUTH

CAISTER ST EDMUND
VILLAGE OFF A47, 3 MILES (5KM) S OF NORWICH

CASTLE RISING
VILLAGE OFF A149, 4 MILES (6KM) NE OF KING'S LYNN

Castle Rising Castle
TEL: 01553 631330

gazetteer

CASTLE RISING

The mighty 12th-century keep of Castle Rising

regularly toured around the area. It is more likely that Isabella's long sojourn at Castle Rising was her own choice, and that living out her days in the quiet peace of Norfolk was her penance for her part in the brutal murder of her husband.

There is much to interest the visitor to Castle Rising. As late as the 18th century, paintings of the castle show ships in the background, for when the castle was built in the 12th century it was near the sea, or at least accessible from the sea. No visitor to Castle Rising can fail to notice the massive Norman earthworks that surround the castle. Great ditches and mounds were thrown up, with walls added later, and still today – even without the threat of archers sending out hails of arrows – the grassy earthworks are difficult to scale.

The mighty, square keep was built between 1138 and 1140, although alterations to entrances and fireplaces were carried out later, and several rooms remain in excellent condition. They include a handsome wall passage and a chapel, complete with a small wall cupboard, on one of the upper floors. There is a well in the basement of the main tower and another in the castle grounds.

Open all year, daily. Closed Xmas and New Year.

CASTLE ACRE

Walk

A fascinating walk through water meadows and along tracks and lanes linking the ruins of castle and priory.

Grid ref: TF816150

INFORMATION

The shorter walk is about 3 miles (5km), the longer about 4½ miles (7km).
Mostly level easy ground though there are some gentle hills.
About 1 mile (1.5km) of road walking, mostly along a wide (sometimes rough) verge.
Several stiles.
Pubs and a café in the village.
Suitable picnic sites at the castle and by the ford.
Toilets at entrance to Priory.

START

Castle Acre is about 4 miles (6.5km) north of Swaffham just off the A1065. Turn off the main

The lovely ruins of Castle Acre Priory in a rural setting by the river road at the hamlet of Newton. There is room for parking in the village, but take care not to cause inconvenience. The walk starts from the church, towards the western end of the village.

DIRECTIONS

From the main gate of the church walk away from the village, and at the end of the churchyard wall turn left down South Acre Road.

WHAT TO LOOK OUT FOR

The castle mound has some interesting plants, native to the chalk which forms the basis of the mound. The tall yellow candelabra-like flower heads of the woolly mullien, a plant largely confined to East Anglia, can be seen in July. There are trout in the River Nar, best spotted from the bridge by the ford.

Continue down to the River Nar. Just before the river, turn left over a stile, then follow a gravel path by the river towards a bridge. Climb a stile to the left of the bridge onto the road, then turn left. After about 200yds (183m) turn right down Cuckstool Lane. At a break in the hedge on the left, enter the castle remains. Walk up the hill, keeping the boundary hedge on your right, and at the top, just before the road, turn right over a stile. Follow a path into a field keeping the houses on your left. Cross the next stile and bear left, keeping the houses on the left. Cross another stile by a horse chestnut tree and walk down a gravel path on to the road.

For the shorter walk, cross over at this point and go down North Street, opposite, continuing to St James Green; continue directions at * below. (For a longer walk turn right and after about 300yds (275m) take a track up on the left for about ¼ mile (0.5km). Keep right and walk across the

27

Walk

CASTLE ACRE

The River Nar at Castle Acre

At the bottom of the hill bear left. Continue uphill on the track for about ½ mile (1km) to join a road, then turn right and follow the road, bearing left by the drive down to the priory. The start point is a short distance further on.

The Castle and the Priory

Castle Acre is a marvellous ruin, standing high above the River Nar. It is also on the line of a Roman road, The Peddars Way.

The castle was built in the 11th century but all that survives are the massive earthworks and the Bailey Gate, which forms an impressive entrance into the centre of the village.

The Priory, also dating from the 11th century, lies in a beautiful setting down by the river at the other end of the village. After the dissolution of the monasteries in 1537 it fell into decay, but despite the plundering of its stone, it remains a most spectacular ruin.

common, crossing a small ford and then, after 100yds (91.5km), take the right-hand track. At the road turn left and walk back towards the village, bearing right at the second road junction to reach St James Green.)

*At the crossroads turn right. At the next junction, turn right by Rose Cottage. Continue along the wide verge until the next road junction then turn left.

After just over ½ mile (1km), pass a manor house on the right, then turn left down a track.

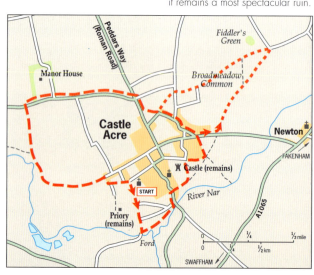

28

CAWSTON—CLEY-NEXT-THE-SEA

Gazetteer

Cawston boasts a splendid 15th-century church and the curious Duelling Stone. This great stone ball, mounted on a plinth and standing at the side of the road, commemorates a duel fought in 1698 between two men over heated words during an election campaign. One was killed, and the other fled to Holland and was later acquitted.

The name is pronounced to rhyme with "why". It is not next to the sea any more, and has not been since the reclaiming of the marshland for pasture in the 17th century left it a mile or so inland. In earlier days Cley was an important port at the mouth of the River Gleven, ranking second only to King's Lynn on this coast. Wool and later cloth was exported to the Netherlands, and the boats brought Dutch tiles back. There is still a small quay on the Gleven, but Cley's most notable feature today is the tremendous 18th-century windmill, with its sturdy brick tower, soaring white sails and conical wooden cap. One of the most photographed windmills in the country, it has been turned into a private house and there has recently been some concern about its preservation. Among attractive houses of flint and brick in the village is the unusual Whalebone House, with panels of flint in the walls framed by whalebones. To the south, where the old harbour stood, the Church of St Margaret is one of Norfolk's finest, rebuilt on a grand scale in the 14th century and a witness to Cley's prosperity at the time. The Black Death in the 1340s caused the money to run short, and so there is a much smaller chancel than the ample nave you might be led to expect. The two-storey 15th-century porch has fantastic battlements and a fan-vaulted roof, whose

CAWSTON
VILLAGE ON B1145, 4 MILES (6KM) SW OF AYLSHAM

CLEY-NEXT-THE-SEA
VILLAGE ON A149, 4 MILES (6KM) NW OF HOLT

The 18th-century windmill at Cley

29

gazetteer

CLEY-NEXT-THE-SEA

BLAKENEY POINT

A minor road runs northwards from Cley through the marshes to Cley Eye on the coast. From here there is a walk of 3 miles (5km) or so over the narrow shingle spit to the nature reserve at Blakeney Point, which belongs to the National Trust. It is a place of lonely and eerie beauty, a magnet to both botanists and birdwatchers, with its mud flats and salt marshes, sandy hillocks and hollows, and spreading lawns of sea lavender. There is a colony of seals here in the winter, terns innumerable nesting in summer with oystercatchers, redshank and other birds, and migrants coming through in the spring and autumn. Blakeney Point can also be reached by boat from Blakeney Quay or Morston.

Blakeney Point, a haven for birdwatchers

bosses are carved with angels and flowers and a woman throwing her distaff at a fox to scare it away from her chickens. The church has numerous fire brasses, including those of John Symonds and his wife in their burial shrouds, with the ominous words 'Now Thus', and their eight children. The transepts had been in ruins since Tudor days. Cley is on the part of the North Norfolk coast known to geologists as the North Alluvial Plain, a strip of land along the sea's edge, not more than 2 miles (3km) deep and built up over the last thousand years by

CLEY-NEXT-THE-SEA

gazetteer

VISITORS TO CLEY
In addition to its human visitors, Cley plays host to large numbers of migrant birds during spring and autumn. Many of these are common species but birds like white-rumped sandpiper, slender-billed gull and rock sparrow are just some of the more unusual species that have turned up in the past few years. Cley is also Britain's most legendary site for vagrant birds, because of its position, protruding into the North Sea.

sediment brought down by the rivers. Local landowners and farmers helped to create it by building walls and digging ditches to transform the salt-marshes into pastureland. The landscape mingles cattle pasture with salt-marshes through which creeks wind their way muddily to the sea among banks of shingle and sand. Birds haunt the area in multitudes, and almost the entire coastline is protected by nature reserves.

(See also Activities, page 92.)

Walk

CLEY MARSHES

Cley Marshes, a block of reed-beds, lagoons and pools is exceptionally good for wading birds and other marshland species. The coast is renowned for its migrants in the spring and, especially, in the autumn. Blakeney Point is famous for rare migrants and good for sea views and salt-marsh.

Grid ref: TG049452

INFORMATION
This attractive walk is approximately 3 miles (5km), or 7 miles (11km) for the longer route. The walking is generally level, but with some shingle to negotiate, especially on the Blakeney Point section.

START
The walk begins at The Eye car park, north of Cley village, along a side road towards the sea wall.

Looking back across the creek towards Cley village

DIRECTIONS
At the western side of The Eye car park, above the road-end, is a grassy bank with a path along the top. This is the West Bank, separating the reclaimed marsh from the saltings. Turn left along the path and follow it towards Cley village.

Continue along the West bank. The West Bank follows the road, with a narrow ribbon of reeds between the two. Opposite the small pool and sluice-gate it is a good idea to descend and follow the road, but if you have boots you can carry on a little further, until the bank angles westwards, then drop down to the road.

Turn left (away from the village) where the beach road meets the main coast road. Cars are not usually travelling fast, but take care and try to keep on the grass verge.

A path above a car park on the right leads up to a Norfolk Naturalists Trust visitor centre, from where a permit may be bought to use the hides dotted around the marsh, which is well worth while. Continue along the roadside. Off the road are several public hides which give better views over the marshes. After ¾ mile (1km) of road-walking you approach a scrub-covered hillside (Walsey Hills) with a reed-fringed pool (Snipes Marsh) on the right.

There is a small car park on the left side of the road, just before Snipes Marsh, and next to it is another grassy bank leading towards the sea. This is the East Bank – one of the best-known bird watching spots in Britain. Walk along the path on top of the bank.

To the right are grazing marshes, to the left is the Naturalists Trust reserve, of reed beds and associated drains and channels. Many people walk straight along the East Bank, to reach either the reserve hides or the sea wall, but one of the most successful strategies can be to sit for a while in the grass and wait for the birds to fly over.

CLEY MARSHES

Towards the end of the East Bank pass Arnold's Marsh, on the right.

At the end of the East Bank, turn left and walk either along the top of the sea wall or at its base. The sea is sometimes worth watching for shearwaters and skuas, but it is less tiring to walk close to the marsh where the shingle is firmer underfoot.

Continue along the sea wall towards the coastguard tower, passing a stile to the Naturalists Trust hide and a small brackish pool with a wartime pillbox beside it. Return to the car park.

7. The second, optional part of the walk now leads west along Blakeney Point. To walk the 8 miles (13km) to the end of the Point and back needs considerable time and energy, and is only recommended if you are fit and motivated.

(A 1½–2 hour boat trip from Blakeney to Morston Quay is an enjoyable alternative in the summer, to see the tern colonies and the seals.) The Hood – about half-way along the Point – is as far as you really need to go.

Return from The Hood along the landward side of the ridge (the

The Church of St Margaret at Cley is one of Norfolk's finest

first landfall for birds on the move); yellow horned poppy and sea kale grow here. A path between the shingle and the mud offers an easier return route back to the car park at The Eye.

 WHAT TO LOOK OUT FOR

Each season brings different varieties of birds to view. August brings waders from the Arctic, September produces wrynecks and other European migrants heading south, as well as seabirds passing along the coast, and there is a special buzz of excitement in October as waifs and strays from Siberia make their first landfall.

Apart from the excitement of autumn, the best time to visit Cley is probably in late May or June, when avocets are nest building, bitterns are booming, and terns and waders are passing up and down the shore.

COCKLEY CLEY–CROMER

COCKLEY CLEY
VILLAGE OFF A1065, 4 MILES
(6KM) SW OF SWAFFHAM

A charming hamlet (pronounced 'Cly') with a reconstructed Iron Age village.

Iceni Village and Museum
TEL: 01760 721339 & 245888

A village of the Iceni tribe has been reconstructed here, as it was 2,000 years ago, on the site where it is believed there was an encampment. There is also a museum in a 15th-century cottage forge, with models and exhibits of local life from prehistoric times to the present day; and there is a museum of agricultural equipment, vintage engines and carriages. The nearby flint church dates back to around AD 630. There is also a nature trail and picnic area.
  Open Apr–Oct, daily.

COLTISHALL
VILLAGE ON B1354, 8 MILES
(13KM) NE OF NORWICH

The village name is synonymous with its nearby airfield which played an important role during World War II. Coltishall has a long history and was notable even when the Doomsday Book was compiled. It has several fine Georgian houses and was for 250 years a centre of the malting industry. In the past many 'Norfolk Wherries' were built here; at one time it was possible for boats to navigate upstream as far as Aylsham, but now the limit of navigation is just south of the village. A couple of public houses are attractively set overlooking the green and River Bure.

CROMER
TOWN ON A140, 21 MILES
(34KM) N OF NORWICH.

In 1779, a bathing machine was advertised at Cromer, and soon the rich Norwich banking families of Gurney and Barclay and their Quaker relations began to take holidays here, and to rent or buy houses. The resort developed further in the 19th century. The sandy beach was an attraction, and so (it was said) were the 'simple manners of the inhabitants', the fact that the sun could be seen both rising and setting in the sea, and the local dressed crab. It was a place for gentlefolk, and there was opposition when the railway arrived in 1877. Hotels and lodging houses now proliferated, the journalist Clement Scott publicised this stretch of coast as 'Poppyland', and a new pier and bandstand were built in the 1900s. The earlier Cromer was a fishing village which took the place of an earlier one still, called Shibden, that was consumed by the sea. The impressive Church of St Peter and St Paul, whose 160-ft (49-m) tower is much Norfolk's tallest, was built in the 14th century. Nearby cottages have been turned into a museum of the area's history and natural history. There is a lifeboat museum, too, and a richly old-fashioned seaside follies show still packs them in at the pier theatre throughout the summertime.

Cromer's sandy beach

34

CROMER–EAST DEREHAM

The museum is housed in five 19th-century fishermen's cottages, one of which has period furnishings. There are pictures and exhibits from Victorian Cromer, with collections illustrating local natural history, archaeology, social history and geology.
   Open all year, daily.
   Closed Good Fri, Xmas period & 1 Jan.

Cromer Museum
EAST COTTAGES, TUCKER ST.
TEL: 01263 513543

The museum in No 2 boat house at the bottom of The Gangway covers local lifeboat history and the RNLI in general. Also of interest is the Lifeboat Station on the pier, where a lifeboat has been stationed since 1804. The history of Cromer from 1804 to the present day is shown together with models of lifeboats. The museum will be housing the recently acquired lifeboat *The H F Bailey* which served on the station from 1935 to 1945 and which saved 518 lives. Also at the museum are 'The Blogg medals'.
   Open May–Oct, daily.

Lifeboat Museum
TEL: 01263 512503

The name comes from an Anglo-Saxon word meaning 'standing water', so the pretty mere in the centre of this town is probably quite ancient. A pleasing jumble of Tudor, Georgian and Victorian houses surrounds the mere, while narrow streets lead up the hill to the market square. Diss stands in the beautiful Waveney Valley.

DISS
TOWN OFF A1066, 19 MILES
(31KM) SW OF NORWICH

Once a horse-market town, Downham Market still retains an air of bustle and activity. Handsome buildings of Carr (or iron) stone line the streets, some of them, such as Dial House in Railway Road, dating from the 1600s. An elegant cast-iron clock tower adorns the market place, and the church has an 18th-century glass chandelier.

DOWNHAM MARKET
TOWN ON A1122, 10 MILES
(16KM) S OF KING'S LYNN

This thriving market town is usually just called Dereham and lies at the heart of Norfolk. A milestone just off the market place claims that London is 100 miles away. The poet William Cowper is buried in the quiet churchyard.
   There is a varied collection of fine Georgian buildings in the market place, modern shop fronts and large maltings. Bishop Bonner's Cottage, with attractive pargeting, stands near the church, a reminder of how Dereham would have been in the 16th century. The Bishop sent many Protestants to the stake under Queen Mary.
   St Withburga, daughter of the Anglo-Saxon King Anna, who founded a convent here in the 7th century, was buried in the churchyard, and miracles followed. The Abbot of Ely later desecrated her grave, and the spring which gushed from it is known as St Withburga's Well.

EAST DEREHAM
TOWN ON A47, 16 MILES
(26KM) W OF NORWICH

35

Walk

EAST HARLING

FOREST RIDES AT EAST HARLING

This pleasant ramble through Forestry Commission rides has the added variety of a river and some open pasture land, the whole walk providing a great deal of wildlife interest.

Grid ref: TL967837

INFORMATION
This walk is about 2½ miles (4km) long.
Level, easy ground.
Some road walking.
No stiles.
Dogs should be kept on leads
Pub in East Harling about 2½ miles (4km) away.
Grassy picnic area at the start.

An old bridge over the River Thet at West Harling Common

START
This walk starts about 5 miles (8km) east of Thetford at West Harling picnic site. From the A1066 turn onto a minor road towards East Harling, then look for signs to the picnic area. There is plenty of room for parking here.

DIRECTIONS
From the picnic site, walk away from the road along a wide ride which is bordered by a mix of beech, oak, sycamore and pine. Keep on this track for about 1 mile (1.5km), ignoring tracks to the right and left, then, when a rough field appears on the left, take the next sandy track to the right, with a field on the left and beech hedge on the right.

(Alternatively it is worth continuing straight on for ¼ mile (0.5km) passing an old cottage on the left until reaching an old bridge with a clear flowing river. Retrace your steps back to the turning).

After a few hundred yards the sandy track bears to the right, but continue straight on along a grassy track, passing some farm buildings on the right.

Just before a gate into a pasture turn right along a path between two fences, then into a field.

EAST HARLING

Walk

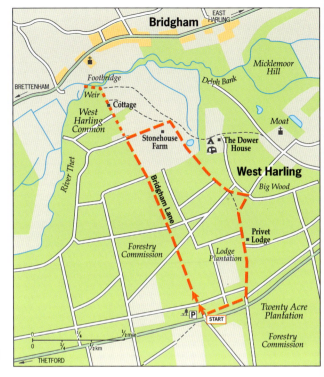

Continue, with the fence on your left, to re-enter the forest. Follow the forestry ride and at a junction of four tracks continue straight on. Shortly afterwards, at a second major crossing of paths, turn right – do watch out here for cars and caravans on their way to the caravan site.

Continue along this track to the road, then turn right to return to the picnic site in about ¼ mile (0.5km).

Breckland

For centuries Breckland was largely an open area with few trees – it largely consisted of wide, open heaths and ploughed land, which, in times of low farm prices, went out of cultivation.

After World War I large parts of Breckland were bought and planted with conifers by the newly formed Forestry Commission, whose remit was to make Britain more self-sufficient in timber.

Breckland heath is a habitat unique to this part of Britain. Many of the plants only occur here, and stone-curlews – strange, nocturnal waders – have their stronghold in this part of East Anglia.

Afforestation and ploughing of the land are considered serious threats to the survival of this fragile ecosystem.

East Harling

The Church of St Peter and St Paul's has two fine monuments; one to Sir Thomas Lovell, the other to Robert Harling, who died at the siege of Paris in 1435. He so much wanted to be buried here that he had his body stewed to preserve the bones that were then carried back to the village on the back of his favourite charger.

WHAT TO LOOK OUT FOR

In summer the wide forest rides support a colourful range of wild flowers including harebell, the tall blue spikes of viper's bugloss, lady's bedstraw, wild mignonette, field scabious and dark mullein.

It is possible to see many species of butterfly including speckled wood, holly blue, gatekeeper and meadow brown. Roe and muntjac deer frequent the forest and are most likely to be seen early and late in the day.

The autumn colours are wonderful here, and this is a good time of year to see the many varieties of fungi which grow under trees. Early March brings masses of snowdrops.

Gazetteer

ECCLES–ERPINGHAM

Remains of the church on the beach at Eccles

ECCLES
LOCATION OFF *B1159*, 10 MILES (16KM) *E* OF NORTH WALSHAM

The village's name probably comes from the Latin word for a church, *ecclesia*, and it is thought that a church may have been constructed here originally far back in Roman times, soon after Constantine the Great's edict of toleration in AD 313. This stretch of the Norfolk coast with its flat, sandy shore is particularly at risk from the sea, which invaded it regularly all through the 17th and 18th centuries. Defences were built of faggots, stones and clay, but it was not enough to save Eccles. The ruthless sea finally claimed the old village and its church of St Mary a hundred years ago. By 1858 the high tides swirled almost up to the tower of the church, which was partly buried in sand. In January 1895 a great storm finally destroyed the church completely, and all that is left now are tumbled boulders of flint masonry, lying on the beach as melancholy fragments of a lost past. The sand dunes above the beach have been planted with marram grass, to knot the dunes into a natural sea wall as protection against further encroachment by the waves. Behind this uncertain barrier are the few bungalows and beach chalets of the present-day Eccles on Sea.

ERPINGHAM
VILLAGE OFF *A140*, 3 MILES (5KM) *N* OF AYLSHAM

The mighty Church of St Mary the Virgin stands on Gallows Hill overlooking the village. Shakespeare wrote about Thomas Erpingham in *Henry V*.

FAKENHAM—FELBRIGG

Straddling the River Wensum, Fakenham is an attractive country town with 18th-century brick houses clustered around its fine market place. The old corn mill, beside the mill race, is now the Old Mill hotel with rooms overlooking the pond. There is a large church with colourful Victorian stained glass. Near by is Thorpland Hall (not open), a Tudor wool merchant's mansion.

(See also Pensthorpe Waterfowl Park & Nature Reserve, page 72.)

A pretty village with a large medieval church, and the splendid Jacobean Felbrigg Hall. Nearby Felbrigg Great Wood is a belt of ancient beech trees.

Felbrigg is a 17th-century house built on the site of an existing medieval hall. In 1969 the last squire, Robert Wyndham Ketton-Cremer bequeathed the entire estate and its contents to the National Trust. The Hall contains a superb collection of 18th-century furniture, pictures and an outstanding library. There are 27 rooms to visit. The walled garden was first established in the 18th century, an octagonal dovecote containing 900 nesting niches was built in the 1750s and fully restored in 1937. A nursery was first established in 1676 with many varieties of trees; this later became the 550-acre (223-ha) wood which shelters the house from the North Sea. There are various events on throughout the season; please telephone for details.

Open: House; Late Mar–early Nov, most afternoons. Garden opens 11am. Park walks daily dawn–dusk.

FAKENHAM
TOWN OFF A148, 23 MILES (37KM) NW OF NORWICH

FELBRIGG
VILLAGE OFF A148, 2 MILES (3KM) S OF CROMER

Felbrigg Hall
TEL: 01263 837444

Felbrigg Hall

FILBY–GREAT WITCHINGHAM

FILBY
VILLAGE ON A1064, 5 MILES
(8KM) NW OF GREAT
YARMOUTH

Pretty Broadland village with a traditional 17th-century Norfolk pub. Filby Broad is a beautiful stretch of water easily accessible by road.

FLEGGBURGH: THE VILLAGE
AT BURGH ST MARGARET,
VILLAGE ON A1064, 4 MILES
(6KM) NE OF ACLE
TEL: 01493 369770

Set in over 35 acres (14ha) of countryside, this reconstruction of a 19th-century town has a working sawmill, a steam engine ride and live shows including the Compton-Christie organ. Other attractions take in vintage vehicles, a narrow gauge railway, peacocks, farmyard animals and traditional crafts.
   Open Etr–Oct, daily.

FRITTON
VILLAGE ON A143, 6 MILES
(10KM) SW OF GREAT
YARMOUTH

Fritton Lake is an attractive tree-fringed mere (but duck decoying is no longer practised here). Oak trees line Fritton Common, famous for its cuckoos.

GELDESTON
VILLAGE OFF A143, 3 MILES
(5KM) NW OF BECCLES

The head of navigation on the River Waveney is Geldeston Lock and this is where The Locks public house is located. Access to the pub is via boat or by a track; beer once had to be brought in by boat. The village lies half a mile north of Geldeston Lock where the 16th-century Wherry public house is located. A pleasant riverside walk along the north bank of the River Waveney leads from Geldeston Lock to Beccles.

GLANDFORD
VILLAGE ON B1156, 3 MILES
(5KM) NW OF HOLT

An internationally known shell museum is one of the attractions of this pleasant cluster of flint and red-brick houses.

GOODERSTONE
VILLAGE OFF A134, 4 MILES
(6KM) E OF STOKE FERRY

The village is noted for its beautiful water gardens, complete with meandering grassy paths, nature walks and an aviary.

GREAT WITCHINGHAM
HAMLET OFF A1067, 2 MILES
(3KM) S OF REEPHAM

Lying to the north of the River Wensum, this pleasant village has a disused mill, some excellent fishing, and Elizabethan Great Witchingham Hall.

**Norfolk Wildlife Centre &
Country Park**
TEL: 01603 872274.

This wildlife park offers a large collection of British and European wildlife. The animals can be viewed in semi-natural surroundings set in 40 acres (16ha) of beautiful parkland. Britain's only team of trained reindeer pull their wheeled sledge around the park, and there are tame animals to entertain both young and old. There are also exciting Commando play areas, a narrow gauge steam railway and a model

GRESSENHALL

farm with numerous rare breeds, most of them tame enough to touch, with a medieval dovecote as the centrepiece and a carp pool.
Open Late Mar–Oct, daily.

This museum portrays the history of Norfolk over the past 200 years. Housed in what used to be a workhouse, it has displays on all aspects of rural life, with special emphasis on agriculture, rural crafts and village life, with working reconstructions. Audio guides are available for interested visitors.

Union Farm is a typical small mixed farm of the 1920s with heavy horses and rare breeds of sheep, cattle, pigs and poultry. There is a nature trail to follow around the farm, which should appeal to children.
Open early Apr–Oct, daily.

**GRESSENHALL
NORFOLK RURAL LIFE
MUSEUM & UNION FARM**
AT GRESSENHALL, VILLAGE OFF B1146, 2 MILES (3KM) NW OF EAST DEREHAM
BEECH HOUSE TEL: 01362 850563.

Coypu at the Norfolk Wildlife Centre, Great Witchingham

41

gazetteer

GREAT YARMOUTH

GREAT YARMOUTH
TOWN ON A47, 18 MILES
(29KM) E OF NORWICH

AT HOME IN A BOAT
Charles Dickens visited Yarmouth in 1848, and the town appears in scenes in David Copperfield (which came out in the following year), among them the dramatic shipwreck in which the villain, Steerforth, loses his life. Earlier in the story, Peggotty, the young David's nursemaid, takes him to her Yarmouth home in a superannuated boat with a door and windows cut in the sides and an iron funnel sticking out for a chimney. This delightful home has a strong fishy smell from the lobsters and crabs in the outhouse, 'in a state of wonderful conglomeration with one another'.

Great Yarmouth Pier and beach

Like the Alde to the south, the River Yare heads for the sea – through the spreading sandflats and mudflats of Breydon Water – only to be deflected to the south by a narrow spit of land. It was on this peninsula that the port of Yarmouth developed, along the river with its back turned firmly to the sea. Here the herring drifters landed their catches and the curing houses smoked the celebrated Yarmouth bloaters. Yarmouth was an active shipbuilding centre, but for centuries its prosperity rested mainly on the vast shoals of herring in the North Sea. Merchants from all over Western Europe and Scandinavia came to the medieval Free Herring Fair, which lasted for 40 days from

42

GREAT YARMOUTH

St Michaelmas. Before World War I more than a thousand fishing boats plied from Yarmouth, but overfishing eventually took its toll and the port turned to servicing North Sea oil and gas operations. There are also regular ferries to Holland, for Yarmouth is 20 miles (32km) nearer to Rotterdam than it is to London. Running inland from the quayside were the old, cramped alleys and courtyards called The Rows, so narrow that a special horse-drawn vehicle called a troll cart, 12 feet (4m) long and only 3 feet (1m) wide, was developed for moving goods in town. Originally dating from medieval times, in 1804 they were numbered, from Row 1 to Row 145. Yarmouth was badly damaged by bombing during World War II, but parts of The Rows survived, and the Old Merchant's House and Row 111 Houses (English Heritage) are open to the public. Sections of the medieval town walls also survive, and along the river quays are examples of merchants' houses from Tudor to Victorian times,

GREAT YARMOUTH

including the grand 18th-century mansion of John Andrews, the herring king, which later became the Customs House. The 13th-century Tollhouse, with its dungeons, is a museum of local history, and the Elizabethan House is now a museum of 19th-century home life. Another interesting building is the Tudor House where Anna Sewell, the author of Black Beauty, was born. Yarmouth today is Norfolk's largest town and East Anglia's most popular seaside resort. It turned around to face the sea in the 19th century, to exploit its miles of sandy beach. The two piers date from the 1850s, and the 'Northern Margate' is fully equipped with amusement arcades, funfair rides, bowling greens, seafront gardens and lively entertainment. The Maritime Museum for East Anglia, in a former home for shipwrecked seamen, deals with the area's maritime past, and a statue of Britannia crowns the 144-ft (44-m) Nelson's Monument.

Elizabethan House Museum
4 SOUTH QUAY
TEL: 01493 855746

A wealthy merchant built this house in 1596. Although it has a late Georgian front, it contains 16th-century panelled rooms, one with a magnificent plaster ceiling. Other rooms have features from later periods, some containing their contemporary furniture and exhibits illustrating domestic life in the 19th-century. Also find children's toys, Lowestoft porcelain and a collection of 18th- and 19th-century glasses.
Open Etr fortnight; Sun before Whitsun–Sep most days. Building work being carried out could affect dates the museum is open; telephone before visiting.

Maritime Museum For East Anglia
MARINE PDE
TEL: 01493 842267

The sea and the fishing industry have played an enormous part in East Anglia's history, and this museum covers all aspects. There are displays on the herring fishery the wherry, life-saving and oil and gas in the North Sea.
Open Etr fortnight, Sun before Whitsun–end Sep, most days.

Merrivale Model Village
WELLINGTON PIER GARDENS,
MARINE PDE
TEL: 01493 842097

Set in attractive landscaped gardens, this comprehensive miniature village is built on a scale of 1:12. The layout includes a 2½-in gauge model railway, radio-controlled boats, and over 200 models set in 1 acre (0.5ha) of landscaped gardens. There are additional amusements, children's rides and remote-controlled cars. During the summer, from June to October, the gardens are illuminated after dusk.
Open Etr–Oct daily.

Museum Exhibition Galleries
CENTRAL LIBRARY, TOLHOUSE ST
TEL: 01493 858900

A regularly-changing series of travelling exhibitions are displayed in the library. Also exhibitions of local art, crafts and other activities.
Open (when exhibition showing) most days. Closed Sat 12.30–1.30, Etr, late May & Aug BH wknds, Xmas & New Year.

44

GREAT YARMOUTH  Gazetteer

This museum is actually in two 17th-century Row Houses, a type of building unique to Great Yarmouth, containing original fixtures and displays of local architectural fittings salvaged from bombing in 1942–3. Near by are the remains of a Franciscan friary, with a rare vaulted cloister, accidentally discovered during bomb damage repairs.

Open Apr–Sep, certain days.

This late 13th-century building was once the town's court house and gaol and has dungeons which can be visited. The rooms above contain exhibits on local history. The museum has become a brass rubbing centre and has a wide range of replica brasses from which rubbings can be made. The reasonable prices for this include materials and instructions.

Open Etr fortnight (Closed Good Fri); Sun before Whitsun–Sep, most days.

Old Merchant's House
ROW 111 (FOLLOW SIGNS TO DOCK AND SOUTH QUAY)
TEL: *01493 857900*

Tollhouse Museum
TOLLHOUSE ST
TEL: *01493 858900*

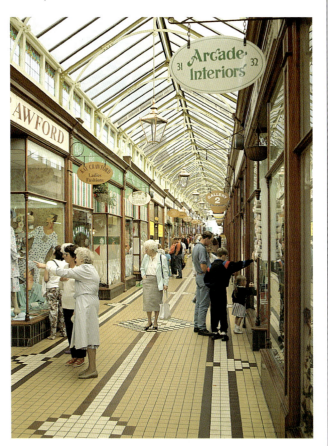

The Central Arcade, Great Yarmouth

45

HEACHAM—HOLME NEXT THE SEA

HEACHAM
VILLAGE OFF A149, 2 MILES
(3KM) S OF HUNSTANTON

The scent of lavender fills the air for miles around the pretty Wash village of Heacham, wafting from the lavender farm at Caley Mill. The American Indian princess Pocahontas is commemorated in a tablet in St Mary's church. She married John Rolfe, squire of Heacham Hall (now demolished), in 1614, and died three years later of smallpox.

Norfolk Lavender
CALEY MILL
TEL: 01485 570384

This is the largest lavender-growing distilling operation in Britain. Different coloured lavenders are grown in strips and harvested in July and August. There are also rose and herb gardens. In summer, there are guided tours of the distillery and gardens, and minibus trips visit a large lavender field.
Open all year, daily. Closed for 2 wks Xmas.

HEYDON
VILLAGE OFF B1149, 3 MILES
(5KM) N OF REEPHAM

Such is the beauty of this little farming village clustered about its green, that at least 30 film and TV productions have been based here. On the north side is an impressive 15th-century Perpendicular church, with wall paintings, a Crusader's shield and, in the clerestory, an original clover-leaf light.
(See also Cycle ride: Blickling Hall and the Marriott Way, page 10.)

HICKLING
VILLAGE OFF A149, 3 MILES
(5KM) E OF STALHAM

This long, winding village near Hickling Broad comprises three communities: Hickling, Hickling Green and Hickling Heath. Hickling Broad is the largest of the Norfolk Broads with an area of 500 acres (202ha). It forms part of a 1,400-acre (567-ha) nature reserve run by the Norfolk Naturalists Trust. Visitors can see a large variety of birdlife from the two nature trails, Deary's Trail and Skoyles Marsh Trail, which both begin at the Warden's House in Stubb Road. (A small fee is charged for each.) Besides migrating birds, the broad is home to the rare swallowtail butterfly.

HINDRINGHAM
VILLAGE OFF A148, 6 MILES
(10KM) NE OF FAKENHAM

Dating back to the Bronze Age, this ancient settlement has some handsome buildings. The sea can be glimpsed 4 miles (6km) distant.

HINGHAM
TOWN ON B1108, 6 MILES
(10KM) W OF WYMONDHAM

In the early 17th century rector Robert Peck left Hingham to seek religious freedom. He and his parishioners founded Hingham, Massachusetts, USA. One of these settlers was Samuel Lincoln, an ancestor of future president Abraham Lincoln. The large market square is fringed by some elegant Georgian and Queen Anne-style houses.

HOLME NEXT THE SEA
VILLAGE OFF A149, 3 MILES
(5KM) NE OF HUNSTANTON

Standing on a wide expanse of windswept beach, the village of Holme also marks the end of the ancient footpath, the Peddar's Way. In Roman times, it was possible to set off from here for ports across the

HOLT–HORNING

Wash and up the east coast. Today, the dunes have many waymarked paths, and there is a small bird sanctuary. Black patches visible in the sea water at Holme are actually the remains of the ancient forest of the North Sea basin.

In 1708 a fire destroyed much of the market town of Holt, but the upside of this is that there are many superb Georgian and Victorian buildings, built to replace the medieval ones. The main street is clean and colourful, and particular attractions include Gresham's School (founded in 1555), the North Norfolk Steam Railway, and Holt Lowes Country Park.

Smooth green lawns sweep down to the waters of the River Bure from thatched boathouses at Horning – considered to be one of the prettiest of the Broadland villages. The main street runs parallel with the river for about a mile and provides the boater with a useful variety of facilities. Local events include the Three Rivers Race, which is held in early June, and the annual regatta in August.

HOLT
SMALL TOWN ON A148, 9 MILES (4KM) W OF CROMER

HORNING
VILLAGE OFF A1062, 3 MILES (5KM) E OF HOVETON

Broadside pub on the River Bure, near Horning

HORSEY–HORSTEAD

Horsey beach

HORSEY
VILLAGE ON B1159, 9 MILES (14KM) NE OF ACLE

Horsey stands on a long, unspoiled beach in what was known as 'devil's country' because of its open wildness. Horsey Mere is especially beautiful, edged by reed beds which still yield reeds for the local inhabitants. The marshes are noted for their wild birds and insects.

Drainage Windpump
TEL: 01493 393904

The windpump mill was built 200 years ago to drain the area, and then rebuilt in 1912 by Dan England, a noted Norfolk millwright. It has been restored since being struck by lightning in 1943.
   Open end Mar–Sep, daily.

HORSHAM ST FAITH
VILLAGE OFF A140, 4 MILES (6KM) N OF NORWICH

A small stream called the Hor ripples through this pretty village which has the ruins of a 12th-century priory and a 15th-century church.

HORSTEAD
VILLAGE ON B1150, 1 MILE (2KM) W OF COLTISHALL

Horstead Mill was burned down in 1963, but visitors can watch the water gushing through its ruins. There are many lovely country footpaths.

HOLKHAM PARK

Cycle ride

*T*his ride offers an excellent day's cycling, exploring the delights of rural North Norfolk. Beginning at the charming little town of Burnham Market, the ride incorporates the magnificent deer park that surrounds Holkham Hall,. a glorious sandy beach, the pilgrimage village of Little Walsingham, and Burnham Thorpe, notable as the birthplace of Lord Nelson.

INFORMATION

Distance
28 miles (45km), with 5 miles (8km) on parkland drives

Difficulty
Moderate

OS Map
Landranger 1:50,000 sheet 132 (North West Norfolk)

Tourist Information
Little Walsingham (summer only), tel: 01328 820510; Hunstanton, tel: 01485 532610

Cycle Hire
Dial House Information Barn (NT), Brancaster Staithe (summer), tel: 01485 210719; Bircham Windmill Cycle Hire, Great Bircham (summer), tel: 01485 578393

Nearest Railway Station
King's Lynn (20 miles/32km)

Refreshments
The splendid Hoste Arms in Burnham Market offers lunches and teas; there is a tea room at Holkham Hall (and excellent picnic spots throughout the Park and at Holkham Beach); pubs and cafés in Walsingham, teas at the Slipper Chapel and in North Creake; a warm family welcome at the unspoilt Lord Nelson pub in Burnham Thorpe.

Abbey ruins, Little Walsingham

HOLKHAM PARK AND THE BURNHAMS

49

Cycle ride

HOLKHAM PARK

HOLKHAM PARK AND THE BURNHAMS

START
Burnham Market is located at the junction of the B1155 and the B1355, just off the A149 coast road between Hunstanton and Cromer, 5 miles (8km) west of Wells-Next-The-Sea. Park carefully along the main street, near the green.

DIRECTIONS
1. Head east away from the church, keeping left through the town along the B1155 towards Well-Next-The-Sea. Turn right through Burnham Overy Town with its mills over the River Burn, and after 1 mile (1.5km) bear right into Holkham Park, signed 'Garden Centre'. Pass the walled Garden Centre, and at the end of the lake keep left, soon to bear right on the estate road that runs in front of the Hall. At a junction turn left (private ahead) and shortly leave the park via gates. Continue through the estate village to the A149 (tea rooms and gallery in Holkham to the right), and cross straight over the main road to follow the access road to the magnificent sandy beach.

2. Retrace your steps back into the Park, to the fork of estate roads beyond the Hall, near the lake. Bear left and proceed through the deer park. Pass the obelisk and gently ascend to gates on the perimeter. Turn left along a lane, go over a crossroads and continue to a further crossroads. Keep straight on, signed 'Wighton', and follow this narrow lane, with good views out to sea, for 2 miles (3km) to reach the B1105 at Wighton.

3. Turn right, then immediately bear off left along the village street, signed 'Binham'. Pass All Saints church and the Sandpiper Inn, then cross the River Stiffkey and shortly bear off right for Great Walsingham. After 1 mile (1.5km) reach the B1388 in the village, turn right, then right again signposted 'Unbridged Ford'.

An old timber-framed house in Little Walsingham

Cross the footbridge over the stream, bear left by the memorial cross into St Peters Road and shortly pass the parish church before joining the B1105 on the edge of Little Walsingham.

4. Turn left into the village centre. Keep left, then turn right at a T-junction, and follow the B1105 through the High Street. Leave the village and after ¼ mile (0.5km) bear off right towards Barsham. Follow this level lane parallel to the River Stiffkey and soon reach the Slipper Chapel. Continue to

HOLKHAM PARK

Cycle ride

HOLKHAM PARK AND THE BURNHAMS

the hamlet of North Barsham, bear right by the green and gradually climb out of the valley on a tiny lane to a crossroads.

5. Go straight over, signposted 'Waterden', pass a chapel on your right, and then turn right for North Holkham. After about a mile go over a crossroads and proceed on a lane through woodland, then take the next lane left, signed 'The Creakes'.

Where the lane curves left, keep straight ahead (unsigned) and descend into North Creake and the B1355. Turn right, and after nearly a mile bear right for Burnham Thorpe.
(To visit the ruins of North Creake Abbey follow the driveway towards Abbey Farm.)
In ½ mile (1km) bear right over the River Burn and soon turn left at a crossroads to pass through Burnham Thorpe. On reaching a T-junction, turn right, then after

Burnham Market's spacious village green is fringed with 18th-century houses

¾ mile (1km) turn right into Burnham Market and keep left at the Lord Nelson pub for the village centre.

Burnham Thorpe is equally peaceful and is beside the River Burn. It was the birthplace in 1758 of Lord Nelson.
  (See also page 22.)

51

Cycle ride

HOLKHAM PARK

The magnificent Holkham Hall

PLACES OF INTEREST

Burnham Market
The largest of seven 'Burnhams' that cluster together along this fine stretch of coastline, this is a handsome little town with a wide green, a small stream flowing across the main road, a collection of fine Georgian houses and St Mary's church.
(See also page 22.)

Holkham Hall
This vast Palladian mansion is one of Britain's most majestic stately homes, situated in lake-watered parkland laid out by 'Capability' Brown in 1762. The house dates from the 18th century and contains a superb hall by William Kent, splendidly appointed state apartments with an impressive art collection and fine furnishings. A Bygones Museum in the adjoining stable block houses an evocative collection of over 4,000 domestic and agricultural artefacts. Open most summer afternoons.
Tel: 01328 710227

Little Walsingham
The village is noted for its medieval history and architecture, and as a place of pilgrimage since 1061. Remains of the Augustinian Priory, the original site of the Shrine of Our Lady, can be seen in the grounds of the new abbey. (See also page 55.)

Slipper Chapel
Built in 1325 as the last wayside chapel for pilgrims before

Walsingham, it was here that the pilgrims took off their shoes and walked the Holy Mile into the village also.

North Creake Abbey
Originally a hospital and almshouse for the poor, it later gained Abbey status. Dissolved in 1506 due to the sudden death by plague of all its inmates, its remains include the 13th-century presbytery and transepts.

WHAT TO LOOK OUT FOR

The fine parkland of Holkham Hall is home to a herd of fallow deer, and Egyptian and Canada geese can be seen on the lake. The plantation of Corsican pines that fronts Holkham Beach is a haven for goldcrests and occasionally crossbills. The neighbouring fields and marshes are feeding grounds for oystercatchers, curlews and lapwings, and in winter flocks of geese are regular visitors. This stretch of coastline is a birdwatcher's paradise.
In early summer the quiet lanes are lined with bright yellow fields of oilseed rape fringed with poppies.
Look out for the sign on nearing Burnham Thorpe directing you to the plaque in the wall, which points out that Nelson was born in the rectory that once stood beyond the wall; it was pulled down in 1803.

HOUGHTON HALL–KING'S LYNN

On 4 July 1729, Sir Robert Walpole, the first Prime Minister of England, had Houghton village demolished and rebuilt elsewhere as 'New Houghton' to improve the view from his magnificent Palladian mansion. The late medieval church was spared, and still stands in the deer park. Sir Robert and his sons (including writer Horace) are buried here.

The beautiful Houghton Hall, with its original William Kent furnishings, and park are open to the public.

Open Apr–Sep, certain afternoons.

HOUGHTON HALL
AT NEW HOUGHTON, HAMLET OFF A148, 1 MILE (2KM) W OF WEST RUDHAM
TEL: 01485 528569

Originally called Bishop's Lynn and in the care of the monasteries, the town's name was changed to King's Lynn by Henry VIII during the Dissolution in the 1530s. This old port on the Great Ouse, several miles inland from the Wash, is a place of character and charm despite its post-war planning. Medieval lanes and alleyways meander back from the quays at the waterfront. The town has many fine buildings, some of which are ancient. The 15th-century St George's guildhall is thought to be the oldest surviving guildhall in England and is owned by the National Trust. A second guildhall – plus two great churches and two marketplaces – testify to King's Lynn's size.

Several early medieval and Tudor warehouses have also survived, while at the southern end of the town stands the splendid 17th-century Hampton Court built by a successful master-baker. The focal point of life in King's

KING'S LYNN
TOWN OFF A47, 39 MILES (63KM) W OF NORWICH

53

KING'S LYNN–LANGLEY GREEN

Lynn is Saturday Market Place with its 13th-century church, St Margaret's. The church is famous for its elaborate 14th-century brasses, Baroque pulpit and 18th-century organ case.

North along the River Ouse is the town's second market square, Tuesday Market with St Nicholas's Church. Between the two market places, on the quay, is the graceful old Custom House. King's Lynn is a romantic town, and visitors wandering through its historic streets will be able to imagine it in former times as a wealthy and active trading community.

Lynn Museum
MARKET ST
TEL: 01553 775001

The geology, archaeology and natural history of the area are the main collections in this local museum. Specimens include an ichthyosaur and a golden eagle. Objects in the archaeology gallery include Bronze Age weapons and the skeleton of a Saxon warrior. Relics from the medieval town of Lynn include an important collection of pilgrim badges. Farm tools, ship models and exhibits from a local fairground machinery firm are also on show.

Open all year, most days. Closed BH, Xmas & New Year.

St George's Guildhall
27 KINGS ST
TEL: 01553 774725

Although it has been used for many purposes, the theatrical associations of this 15th-century Guildhall are strongest: Shakespeare himself is said to have performed here. Its present use as the town's theatre was brought about in the 1950s after an 18th-century theatre, incorporated into the hall, was restored and enlarged. The annual King's Lynn Festival takes place 20 July–3 August.

When not in use as a theatre or cinema open all year, most days. Closed Good Fri, 25–26 Dec & 1 Jan.

Town House Museum of Lynn Life
46 QUEEN ST
TEL: 01553 773450

Opened in 1992, this museum shows the life of merchants, tradesmen and families who made the town a prosperous place. Historic room displays include: costumes, toys, a working Victorian kitchen and a 1950s living room.

Open all year, certain days.

LANGHAM
VILLAGE ON B1388, 2 MILES
(3KM) SW OF BLAKENEY

A lovely village, the pub of which has a fascinating collection of antique shoes. The author of *Mr Midshipman Easy* and *The Children of the New Forest*, Frederick Marryat, farmed here. He is buried in the churchyard.

LANGLEY GREEN
VILLAGE OFF A146, 3 MILES
(5KM) N OF LODDON

Ruins of the 12th-century Premonstratensian monastery, old farms and pretty cottages stand on the edge of the marshes of the River Yare.

LETHERINGSETT–LITTLE WALSINGHAM

Known to many locals as 'Lansett', this beautiful village nestles comfortably in the lovely Glaven Valley, hemmed in by fine old trees and emerald meadows. Many houses are decorated with flint of local pebbles, and the Church of St Andrew has a remarkable 18th-century barrel organ. Letheringsett Hall (not open) is the 18th-century seat of the Cozens Hardy family.

In this attractive Georgian village is Dunham Museum, with imaginative displays of working tools and machinery. In the church, the bases of the pillars form seats.

The shrine of Our Lady of Walsingham has been a pilgrimage site since the 11th century. The spring was said to effect miraculous cures. Virtually every English king from Richard I to Henry VIII journeyed here. Walsingham High Street opens out into a pleasant square in the centre of which is a 16th-century pump house and beacon brazier. Great Walsingham is due north and has beautiful 'poppyhead' pews in the

LETHERINGSETT
Village on A148, 1 mile (2km) W of Holt

LITTLE DUNHAM
Village off A47, 4 miles (6km) NE of Swaffham

LITTLE WALSINGHAM
Small town on B1105, 4 miles (6km) S of Wells-next-the-Sea

The church at Letheringsett

55

LITTLE WALSINGHAM—LONG STRATTON

church. Houghton-in-the Dale, a couple of miles from Walsingham, on the Fakenham road, has a church with an ancient screen. Below the village is the Slipper Chapel, the centre of the Roman Catholic pilgrimage to Our Lady of Walsingham. This beautiful building was where pilgrims took their shoes off before walking on barefoot
(See also Cycle ride: Holkham Park and The Burnhams, page 49.)

Shirehall Museum
COMMON PLACE
TEL: 01328 820510

The museum is in an almost perfect Georgian courtroom with its original fittings, including a prisoner's lock-up. The displays show Walsingham's history, with a special exhibition on the history of pilgrimage. There is also a tourist information centre.
Open Maundy Thu–Sep, daily.

Walsingham Abbey Grounds
TEL: 01328 820259

In the grounds of the Abbey are the ruins of the original Augustinian priory built in the 1100s. The priory was built over the shrine of Our Lady of Walsingham which had been established in 1061. The remains include the east wall of the church, and the south wall of the refectory still intact. These include a window of the Decorated period.
Open Etr–Sep, certain days. Other times contact Estate Office.

LODDON
SMALL TOWN OFF A146, 6 MILES (10KM) NW OF BECCLES

Once a thriving port on the Broads, Loddon now enjoys a rather more relaxed role as a boating centre. A charming marina has pleasure craft bobbing up and down on the River Chet (a tributary of the Waveney). Hardley Flood is an area of flooded marsh providing an important wildfowl site. The town, although expanding, has avoided being spoiled. There are Georgian houses, a market square and the 15th-century Holy Trinity Church, with unusual painted screens, set in a vast churchyard.
The churches of the Southern Broads are mainly Norman buildings, as at the village of Chedgrave, immediately north of Loddon. All Saints Church standing slightly raised above the river contains 16th- and 17th-century stained glass believed to have originated from Rouen Cathedral.

LONG STRATTON
VILLAGE ON A140, 10 MILES (16KM) S OF NORWICH

The village church is one of only two in England to have a Sexton's wheel, a device with counter-rotating wheels for working out holy days. They were used to determine Lady Fast day, which was a movable fast day. Pieces of string were attached by the sexton to six of the fleurs-de-lis of one wheel. Both wheels were set in motion. The day which the string of the one wheel caught in the other, was the day chosen to be observed.

56

LUDHAM MARSHES

Walk

An interesting and easy walk, close to one of the Broadland waterways and providing fine views across traditional grazing marshes.

Grid ref: TG392180

INFORMATION
The walk is about 3 miles (5km) long.
Level ground, but can be very muddy and slippery by marshes; care needed by dykes.
A little road walking on a no-through road.
Dogs should be kept on leads.
Pub offering bar snacks in Ludham, with garden; also café.
Grassy area by staithe for picnics.
Toilets by staithe.

START
Ludham is about 14 miles (22.5km) north-east of Norwich. From Wroxham, take the A1062 to Ludham, continue through the village centre, then shortly afterwards take the turning on the right, signposted 'Womack

Marsh thistle

Staithe'. There is parking on the staithe near the shop and toilets.

DIRECTIONS
From the staithe, walk on down the lane beside the moorings, past some houses on the right, until you come to the 'County Sailing Base'. Immediately on the left-hand side of the Base is a footpath (do not take the track marked 'bridleway' to the left of the footpath). The footpath runs along a low bank, with Womack Water on the right; to the left are extensive marshes. After about ½ mile (1km), at a cottage, the path turns left and then runs alongside the River Thurne, though separated from it by a bank of reeds. After about ¾ mile (1km) chalets can be seen on the far bank, and the path leaves the river by a pumphouse. Cross a dyke on a plank bridge, taking care where it is a little rough, then turn left along a grassy track which is bordered on either side by dykes. After about ¼ mile (0.5km), go through a gate then turn left along another grassy track which is partly bordered by a wood on the right-hand side. In about ¾ mile (1km) the track bears right by a house and emerges to join the outward route by the 'County Sailing Base'. Retrace the route back to the start.

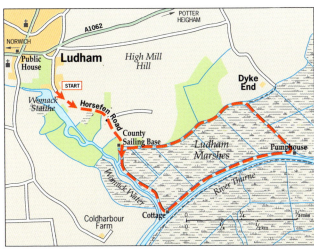

57

LUDHAM MARSHES

Grazing marshes

The grazing marshes in Broadland have traditionally been grazed by cattle during the summer. The rich pastures were particularly good for fattening cattle, and animals were driven down on foot by drovers from as far away as Scotland. The marshes were drained by a system of dykes, and water was returned to the river by pumps – originally wind-powered, then steam-driven and most recently fuelled by diesel. The older methods were the least efficient and consequently the grazing

A drainage channel across the marshland

marshes would frequently flood in winter, providing a marvellous habitat for wildfowl.

In the 1960s and 1970s many of these old grazing marshes were ploughed up to be intensively farmed for cereals, but farmers are now being encouraged to return the land to the more traditional grazing practices. Hopefully, this will prevent the further pollution of the Broads and herald the return of its rich plant and animal life.

WHAT TO LOOK OUT FOR

The dyke systems on the marshes have a rich animal and plant life. A special feature of the area is the Norfolk aeshna dragonfly which is only found on the Norfolk Broads and is now the symbol of the Broads Authority. Redshank and lapwing breed on the grazing marshes. The very tall marsh sow-thistle, also largely confined to the Norfolk Broads, is a feature of the marsh banks in late summer. The remains of an old pump mill stand in the marshes.

MANNINGTON HALL GARDENS—MARTHAM

 Gazetteer

Only 7 miles (11km) from the sea in the open, rolling countryside of North Norfolk is the romantic Mannington Hall. Purchased in the 18th century by the brother of Sir Robert Walpole, the lovely medieval moated house is still owned by the Walpole family. Although the gardens undergo periodic work, there are a number of areas to interest the garden lover, especially the Heritage Rose Garden – a deliciously scented layout – and a wild valley planted with unusual trees.

Walking across the spacious lawns towards the house, it is clear that storms have badly damaged some of the great cedars, but fast-growing wellingtonias have been planted to replace those lost. Inside the Victorian 'battlement' walls, the borders are overflowing with herbaceous plants and roses, with *Rosa* 'Canary Bird' showing its single yellow blooms in late spring. The bed beneath the house wall has peonies and lupins, while on the wall itself is a fine climbing hydrangea, *H. petiolaris*, and opposite is a splendid weeping pear with grey-green leaves.

Around the corner of the house *Rosa banksiae* 'Lutea' climbs vigorously close to a mauve wisteria, while rock roses brighten up the gravel with their pink and white flowers in early summer. A formal rose garden dominated by hybrid teas and with a sundial in the centre is surrounded by juniper. Within the moat an intricate pattern of sweetly scented herbs are planted underneath urns, filled with hyacinths in spring and replaced with brightly coloured pelargoniums later on.

Fruit trees line the intimate enclosure of the Heritage Rose Garden, which is divided into several areas, each representing a period of the rose's historical development. In all there are more than 1,000 different varieties, including a wide range of wild roses. The Medieval Garden has turf seats and some very old roses, including *Rosa gallica* 'officinalis', and *R. spinosissima* near a small yew tree. Beyond the other formal areas of Mannington Hall, which include a tranquil 17th-century knot garden, is a spectacular wild valley. Here, in a totally different mood, there are many fascinating trees, including seven specimens of Acer *palmatum* which are well over 100 years old.

Open Etr–Oct, limited opening.

MANNINGTON HALL GARDENS
AT SAXTHORPE, VILLAGE ON B1149, 6 MILES (10KM) SE OF HOLT
TEL: 01263 584175

This large village has several Georgian houses and shops surrounding its spacious green. A lane near the church leads down to the Martham Ferry where a private swing bridge is normally kept open to allow the passage of boats. Martham Broad, a mile further upstream is a 140-acre (57-ha) nature reserve surrounded by reed and marsh. The River Thurne terminates at West Somerton which is only 2 miles (4km) from the North Sea.

MARTHAM
VILLAGE ON B1152, 3 MILES (5KM) W OF WINTERTON-ON-SEA

MUNDESLEY—NORTH WALSHAM

MUNDESLEY
SMALL TOWN ON B1145, 4 MILES (6KM) NE OF NORTH WALSHAM

After the crumbling cliffs and ragged-edged fields which are being ravaged by the encroaching sea, the long, flat beach at Mundesley is a welcome respite. Bathing is safe, and groynes are set at regular intervals to prevent the sand from being washed away. Pronounced 'Munsley', this pleasing seaside town is unspoilt, but still offers golf, bowling and other facilities.

NEATISHEAD
VILLAGE OFF A1151, 4 MILES (6KM) NE OF WROXHAM

The main street boasts fine late Georgian houses. The village school was founded in 1946 by the Preston family of Beeston Hall; this attractive 18th-century mansion is a mile away. The wooded Limekiln Dyke penetrates westwards from Barton Broad to the centre of Neatishead where there are moorings.

NORTH WALSHAM
TOWN ON A149, 14 MILES (23KM) N OF NORWICH

Becoming prosperous from the woollen cloth trade in medieval times, North Walsham's wealth was further increased by the digging of the North Walsham and Dilham Canal, which connected it to the Broads. There are many handsome Georgian buildings set along attractive winding streets. The grammar school was founded by John Paston in 1606.

NORTH NORFOLK RAILWAY

The 25-minute journey on the North Norfolk Railway might be an eye-opener for those who think of Norfolk as a flat county. For much of the outward journey over the 5¼ miles (8.5km) from Sheringham to Holt, the locomotive has to work hard on gradients as steep as 1 in 80, but the open embankments enable passengers to enjoy the marvellous views over the sea to the north and the woods inland.

Once part of the Midland & Great Northern Railway, the section that forms today's North Norfolk Railway was built to cater as much for holiday traffic as to serve local communities, but the seasonal nature of the line's income led to its downfall. It closed in stages between 1959 and 1964, although a new station at Sheringham can still be reached by train from Norwich and it is only a few minutes' walk between the stations. Re-opened to passengers in 1975, the original Sheringham station reflects the number of passengers it handled when named trains like the *Broadsman* and *Norfolkman* called here. The elaborate cast-iron brackets supporting the canopy are adorned with hanging baskets, and there is plenty to look at while waiting for the next train, including a museum portraying the history of the Midland & Great Northern Railway.

NORTH NORFOLK RAILWAY
AT SHERINGHAM, TOWN ON A149, 4 MILES (6KM) W OF CROMER
TEL: 01263 822045

Ring Haw at Sheringham: the town also has a main line station with services to Norwich

gazetteer

NORTH NORFOLK RAILWAY

After viewing the delightful landscape on the way to Weybourne, passengers will not be surprised to learn that it has been designated an Area of Outstanding Natural Beauty. Once a golf course on the seaward side is left behind, the land on either side is attractive arable country with fields of barley, carrots and sugarbeet. Inland the fields rise up to the woodlands of Sheringham Park, landscaped by Humphry Repton, and regarded by him as his finest work. It is also interesting to see the railway from the park, from a viewpoint which puts the trains into the perspective of a fine panorama of coastline and agricultural hinterland.

The one intermediate station, at Weybourne, offers several reasons to postpone the final leg of the journey to Holt. It is here that locomotives are restored, and guided tours can be arranged by the stationmaster. A board on the station suggests walks through nearby Kelling Woods, and in the opposite direction, 1 mile (1.5km) from the station, is the village of Weybourne. As well as the ruins of an Augustinian priory and windmill, walkers are close to Weybourne Hope where exceptionally deep water made it a likely place for an attempted invasion in 1588 and again during World War II. The section to Holt climbs across Kelling Heath with good views out to sea. Although the station at Holt is yet to be developed, passengers in high season are often met by a horse-bus for conveyance into the Georgian market town. There are a number of streets and shops worth exploring.

Train service: daily Jul–Sep; wknds in May; Sundays in Mar, Apr & Oct; also Etr week.

NORWICH

NORWICH

A sturdy Norman castle frowning down from its vantage point on a hill; a delicate cathedral with a slender spire; crooked cobbled streets and several lively shopping centres are just a few of the many attractions of Norfolk's largest city. Whether the visitor is interested in history, architecture, shopping, art, museums, or leisure activities, Norwich has something to offer.

A great wall four miles (6km) long with a dozen gates once surrounded the city, which originated as three Anglo-Danish settlements by the River Wensum. The castle was built by the Normans about 1160 at the highest point of the small town, and was refaced in the 1830s. For a while it had a grim reputation as the county gaol, but now exists as the Castle Museum. Yet even the presence of British ceramic teapots and some splendid paintings does not detract from the sheer power and dominance that exudes from this formidable fortress.

The textile industry was the most important one in medieval Norwich, led by Flemish weavers who introduced the manufacture of worsted cloth. The resulting wealth that was poured into the city by the Dutch immigrants brought about the building of fine town houses and the construction of churches in the Perpendicular style. Thirty-three medieval churches remain within the old city walls, although not all are now used. Among the best are St John Maddermarket, with its collection of monumental brasses; spacious St Andrew's, dating from 1478; St Michael-at-Plea, which takes its name from the archdeacon's courts; the 18th-century Octagon Chapel, which John Wesley called the most elegant meeting house in Europe; and St Peter Mancroft, which dominates the market place. The Friends Meeting House (1826) was attended by the family of the famous Quaker prison reformer Elizabeth Fry.

NORWICH
CITY ON A11, 98 MILES
(158KM) NE OF LONDON

Norwich Cathedral

63

NORWICH

ELIZABETH FRY
1780–1845. English prison reformer and philanthropist. Elizabeth Gurney came from a Quaker banking family which had a country house, Earlham Hall (now part of the University of East Anglia), outside Norwich and a town house in Gurney Court, off Magdalen Street. Her family attended the Quaker meeting house in Upper Goat Lane, where her voluminous diaries are now kept. She married a London Quaker merchant, Joseph Fry, in 1800 and they lived first in St Mildred's Court in the City and later at East Ham. Visiting Newgate Prison in London, she was horrified by the spectacle of starving and drunken women prisoners and the state of the children; in 1816, therefore, she founded a committee for improving conditions and discouraging immorality.

Bridewell Museum
BRIDEWELL ALLEY
TEL: *01603 667228*

p65, Norwich Cathedral pp66/7, Norwich: Pulls Ferry, swans and cygnets

Outshining all these is the magnificent cathedral, combining sturdy Norman arcades with the soaring splendour of some of the best Gothic architecture in Britain. Norwich's spire is the second highest in Britain after that of Salisbury Cathedral.

Banking was also important to Norwich. The local Gurneys' Bank, established in 1775, joined up with three other country bankers to form Barclays Bank in 1896. The main city branch of the bank, in Bank Plain, has a striking gilded banking hall, and is still called Gurneys' Bank.

Other fine buildings include the Great Hospital, which was founded by Walter de Suffield in 1249 and is centred around the charming Church of St Helen. The old guildhall still stands proudly overlooking the market place, often covered with the brightly coloured awnings of the traders' stalls. Many other attractive buildings can be found unexpectedly down little alleys and in secluded courtyards, away from the bustle of the busy modern city. Norwich has an abundance of cobbled streets, meandering away from the old centre, and it is easy for the visitor to wander at will, enjoying the ancient feel of the city.

There are several museums in Norwich, including the nationally acclaimed Sainsbury Centre for Visual Arts at the University of East Anglia. The Royal Norfolk Regimental Museum and the Strangers' Hall Museum of Domestic Life offer more specific displays. Norwich also has several new shopping malls, and the Mustard Shop is run by Colman's mustard company. The University of East Anglia occupies a pleasant campus in the suburbs.

Built in the late 14th century, this flint-faced merchant's house was used as a prison from 1583 to 1828. It now houses displays illustrating the trades and industries of Norwich during the past 200 years, including a large collection of locally made boots and shoes.

Open all year, most days. Closed Good Fri, Xmas & New Year.

NORWICH   *gazetteer*

65

gazetteer

NORWICH

NORWICH *gazetteer*

 *gazetteer* NORWICH

NORWICH  *gazetteer*

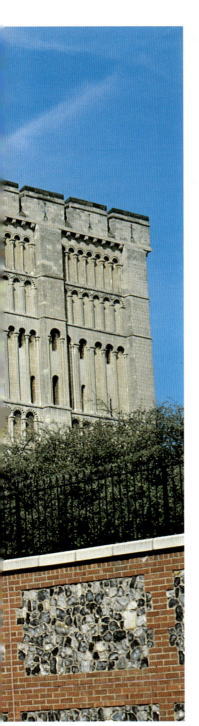

Visitors may visit the Council Chamber and view civic plate and insignia dating from 1549. The civic regalia is on view Mon–Fri 2–3.30, or at other times for parties by arrangement.

Open all year, most days.

Norman Castle Keep built in the 12th century, and museum housing displays of art, archaeology, natural history, Lowestoft porcelain, Norwich silver, a large collection of paintings (with special emphasis on the Norwich School of Painters) and British ceramic teapots. There are also guided tours of the dungeons and battlements.

Open all year, daily. Closed Good Fri, Xmas period & New Year.

Norwich Cathedral is a beautiful Norman building set in the largest close in England. Originally a Benedictine foundation, it possesses the largest monastic cloisters in England and is of great architectural and artistic interest. The special features include: the Saxon bishop's throne, nave bosses depicting scenes from the Bible from the Creation to the Resurrection; the 14th-century Despenser reredos. Services take place several times every day.

Open daily.

Guildhall
GUILDHALL HILL
TEL: *01603 666071*

Norwich Castle Museum
CASTLE MEADOW
TEL: *01603 223624*

Norwich Cathedral
THE CLOSE
TEL: *01603 764385 & 767617 (WEEKENDS)*

Norwich Castle

69

NORWICH

Royal Norfolk Regimental Museum
SHIREHALL
TEL: 01603 223649

The museum displays deal with the social as well as military history of the county regiment from 1685, including the daily life of a soldier. It is housed in an old courtroom of the historic Shirehall. It is linked to the Castle Museum by a tunnel through which prisoners were taken to court. There is also a reconstruction of a World War I communication trench. In World War I, the Norfolk Regiment fielded 20 battalions; 5,000 men were killed, one-third of them on the Somme. One of the most well-known of those killed was actually a woman, the daughter of a Norfolk vicar, Edith Cavell, executed by the Germans in 1915 for helping British officers escape from Belgium. Audio-visual displays and graphics complement the collection. There is a programme of temporary exhibitions.

Open all year, daily. Closed Good Fri, Xmas period & 1 Jan.

Sainsbury Centre for Visual Arts
UNIVERSITY OF EAST ANGLIA
TEL: 01603 456060 & 593199

At Earlham in Norwich's western outskirts, this striking single-span gallery — like a futuristic factory — was designed by Sir Norman Foster in the 1970s for the art collection given to the University of East Anglia by Sir Robert and Lady Sainsbury in 1973. European art of the 19th and 20th centuries is on display together with ethnographical art. You can see African tribal sculpture and Oceanic works along with North American and Pre-Colombian art. Egyptian, Asian and European antiquities are on show. Artists represented include Degas, Picasso, Giacometti, Modigliani, Epstein, Henry Moore and Francis Bacon. There is also a separate Art Nouveau collection. Various other exhibitions are held during the year.

Open all year, most days. Closed BH Mon & University closure at Xmas.

St Peter Hungate Church Museum
PRINCES ST (NEAR ELM HILL)
TEL: 01603 667231

Built in 1460, this fine church has a hammer-beam roof and good examples of Norwich painted glass. It is now a museum of church art and a brass rubbing centre with a wide selection of brasses to rub from; a small charge is made which includes materials and instructions.

Open Etr–Sep, most days.

Strangers' Hall
CHARING CROSS
TEL: 01603 667229

Strangers' Hall, once a medieval merchant's house, contains a series of rooms furnished in period styles from early Tudor to late Victorian. In addition there are displays of toys and games, children's books and domestic life. Changing exhibitions of costume and textiles are shown in one gallery.

Open all year, most days. Closed Good Fri, Xmas period & New Year.

OXBURGH HALL

Oxburgh Hall has its roots firmly in the medieval era. Built for the Bedingfeld family in 1482, it has mellow stone walls rising sheer from the waters of its moat, and a great Tudor gatehouse. But Oxburgh's history is not only a long one, it has also experienced moments of danger and excitement. The fact that the house has survived at all is, indeed, little short of miraculous.

After the Civil War it was ransacked by Cromwell's men who set fire to part of it. Much later, in 1951, financial difficulties beset the family and after 500 years of the Bedingfeld family's occupation Oxburgh Hall was sold to a development company. Three months later that company put it up for auction, with the only prospective buyer being a demolition firm. However, at the eleventh hour, on the morning of the sale, Lady Bedingfeld raised enough money to make a successful bid and bought the house back.

There are portraits of the Bedingfeld family throughout the house, and the wonderful 17th-century wall-coverings of embossed and painted Spanish leather on the corridor and stairs are a notable feature. The King's Room, named in honour of a visit by Henry VII in 1497, now contains wall hangings embroidered by Mary, Queen of Scots and Elizabeth, Countess of Shrewsbury.

Open late Mar–Oct, certain days.

OXBURGH HALL
AT OXBOROUGH, VILLAGE OFF A134, 3 MILES (5KM) NE OF STOKE FERRY
TEL: 01366 328258

Moated Oxburgh Hall

PASTON—REEDHAM

PASTON
HAMLET ON B1159, 4 MILES (6KM) NE OF NORTH WALSHAM

Famous for the 'Paston Letters' written during the Wars of the Roses. A straggling village with a noble church and an impressive thatched tithe barn.

PENSTHORPE WATERFOWL PARK & NATURE RESERVE
AT FAKENHAM, TOWN OFF A148, 23 MILES (37KM) NW OF NORWICH PENSTHORPE (SIGNED OFF A1067 NORWICH TO FAKENHAM ROAD) TEL: 01328 851465

Pensthorpe Waterfowl Park is situated in the valley of the River Wensum and covers 200 acres (81 ha) of beautiful Norfolk countryside. Based on old gravel workings, its five lakes are home to the largest collection of waterfowl and waders in Europe. With spacious walk-through enclosures, a network of hard surfaced pathways ensures close contact with birds at the water's edge. In the Courtyard Gallery year-round exhibitions of paintings, wildlife photography and craftwork can be viewed. Leaflets and events information can be obtained by phoning.

Open all year, daily.

RANWORTH
VILLAGE OFF B1140, 4 MILES (6KM) NW OF ACLE

This beautiful and popular small village beside Malthouse Broad is famous for St Helen's Church – often called the 'Cathedral of the Broads'. Those who climb to the top of its tall tower will be rewarded with magnificent views across the surrounding marshes and five Broads. The church is noted for its fine painted screen and 15th-century illuminated choir book.

Navigation is not allowed on the nearby Ranworth Broad as it is a bird sanctuary which forms part of the Bure Marshes Nature Reserve. However, the Norfolk Naturalists Trust has provided a Broadlands Conservation Centre near the entrance to the Broad, housed in a timber and thatched building on a floating pontoon.

REEDHAM
VILLAGE OFF B1140, 6 MILES (10KM) S OF ACLE

An attractive village on rising ground above the River Yare. The Ship and Lord Nelson pubs overlook the river and the Norton Marshes. At the eastern end of the village the railway crosses the river on a swing bridge which is regularly open to allow passage of yachts and larger vessels. A mile (1.5km) west of Reedham, overlooked by the Ferry Inn, is Reedham ferry, the last vehicle ferry running on the River Yare.

Pettitts Animal Adventure Park
OFF A47
TEL: 01493 700094

Farmyard animals – rabbits, goats, ducks – many of which have been hand raised, can be seen here along with more exotic creatures like wallabies, falabella horses, peacocks and chipmunks. The art of feather craft and candle carving are among the crafts which are demonstrated. Daily live entertainment is provided by children's entertainers. Other attractions include the play area, train rides, and vintage car ride. Special events are planned throughout the season.

Open Etr Sun–Oct, most days.

REEPHAM–SNETTISHAM

Gazetteer

Originally, Reepham consisted of three parishes, Hackford, Reepham and Whitwell, belonging to three sisters. Each sister had her own church. Today, there are two churches remaining, in one churchyard. The spacious market square is lined by Georgian properties. Gently undulating countryside surrounds it.

REEPHAM
VILLAGE ON B1145, 6 MILES (10KM) SW OF AYLSHAM

The fine brick undercroft seen in the cloister is one of the most notable features of the ruin of this small Augustinian priory: built in about 1216 it is an exceptionally early use of this material.
  Open any reasonable time.

ST OLAVES PRIORY
AT ST OLAVES, VILLAGE ON A143, 1 MILE (2KM) SW OF FRITTON

Interesting buildings in Scole include the Scole Inn, a huge old coaching inn built in 1655 of red brick, and the 16th-century Crossways hotel.

SCOLE
VILLAGE ON A140, 2 MILES (3KM) E OF DISS

This bustling old fishing village slips easily into its more recent role as a popular holiday resort. Elegant Georgian and Edwardian houses surround the small flint-built fishermen's cottages. Rugged cliffs turn into rolling wooded hills rich in wildlife. Sheringham Park (National Trust) is 770 acres (312ha) of parkland, some of which was landscaped by Sir Humphry Repton. The town also contains the terminus of North Norfolk Railway.

SHERINGHAM
TOWN ON A149, 4 MILES (6KM) W OF CROMER

A lively village which had a World War II airbase. The church has a cupola and one of the finest Tudor wooden lecterns in the world.

SHIPDHAM
VILLAGE ON A1075, 4 MILES (6KM) SW OF EAST DEREHAM

Snettisham has much to offer the visitor. There is a magnificent 14th-century church, which is an unusual shape as the east chancel is missing. The spire soars 175ft (53m) over the village, and features in J P Hartley's *The Shrimp and the Anemone*. Another attraction is Park Farm.

SNETTISHAM
VILLAGE ON A149, 4 MILES (6KM) S OF HUNSTANTON

You can see farming in action here with lambing in the spring, sheep shearing in May and deer calving in June and July. Sheep, goats, lambs, rabbits, turkeys, ducks, chickens, ponies and piglets, can be seen in the paddocks, and the sheep centre has over 40 different breeds. Take a safari ride around the estate to see the magnificent herd of red deer. Other attractions include a large adventure playground, horse and pony rides, several miles of farm trails, visitor centre and craft workshops, including pottery studio and leather worker.
  Open Feb–Dec, daily.

Park Farm
TEL: 01485 542425

73

SOUTH WALSHAM—STRUMPSHAW

SOUTH WALSHAM
VILLAGE ON B1140, 3 MILES
(5KM) NW OF ACLE

South Walsham Broad is just one of many tranquil expanses of reedy water in this region. Lovely South Walsham stands on its tree-fringed banks. This ancient village has the Fairhaven Garden Trust, about 60 acres (24.5 ha) of bird sanctuary on a private broad; the Elizabethan South Walsham Hall (now a hotel); and the 17th-century Ship Inn. There are also two churches sharing one churchyard.

Fairhaven Garden Trust
2 THE WOODLANDS,
WYMERS LN
TEL: 01603 270449

These delightful woodland and water gardens, with a private inner broad, offer peace and tranquillity and a combination of cultivated and wild flowers. In spring there are masses of primroses and bluebells, with azaleas and rhododendrons in several areas. Candelabra primulas and some unusual plants grow near the waterways, which are spanned by small bridges. In summer the wild flowers come into their own, providing habitat for butterflies, bees and dragonflies. There is a separate bird sanctuary for bird watchers. Riverboat trips on the *Lady Beatrice* run from the gardens around the two South Walsham Broads.
Open late Mar–early Oct, most days.

STALHAM
VILLAGE OFF A149, 7 MILES
(11KM) SE OF NORTH
WALSHAM

The ancient market town of Stalham lies at the northern reaches of the Broads on the beautiful River Ant. Boats at South Staithe allow visitors to explore How Hill Water Gardens, the River Ant itself, and nearby Hickling Broad. Composer E J Moeran wrote some evocative music here, based on the haunting waters of the Broads and Stalham Windmill.

STOW BARDOLPH
VILLAGE ON A10, 2 MILES
(3KM) NE OF DOWNHAM
MARKET

Stow Bardolph boasts some handsome houses, a fine park with rolling meadows and proud trees, a lovingly restored hall, and a church with an unusual effigy. Inside a mahogany cupboard is a life-sized, fully-dressed wax model of Sarah Hare, a parishioner of Holy Trinity, complete with warts and staring eyes, who died in 1744 from pricking her finger while sewing.

STRUMPSHAW
VILLAGE OFF A47, 4 MILES
(6KM) SW OF ACLE

Merging with neighbouring Lingwood, Strumpshaw nevertheless has its own distinct character. It is a hill (a rarity in Norfolk) from which Norwich can be seen, and a little 14th-century church. Strumpshaw Fen is an RSPB sanctuary on the River Yare. Covering about 600 acres (243 ha), the reserve exhibits the complete range of Broadland habitats, which can be viewed from its several miles of good footpaths. Hides allow visitors to watch marsh harriers and many other birds.
(See also Activities, page 92.)

Cycle ride

SANDRINGHAM AND HUNSTANTON

*U*sing minor roads and off-road tracks this ride takes in gently rolling quiet countryside. Starting in a seaside town the ride soon takes you away from the traffic and into a superb nature reserve. It continues through villages, all waiting to be explored, and visits a working windmill and the royal estate of Sandringham. A 4-mile (6.5-km) loop to pretty Wolferton is included, but may be omitted if more time is needed in nearby Sandringham.

INFORMATION

Total Distance
28 miles (45km), with 4½ miles (7km) off-road

Difficulty
Easy

The striped cliffs at Hunstanton

OS Map
Landranger 1:50,000 sheet 132 (North West Norfolk)

Tourist Information
Hunstanton, tel: 01485 532610

Cycle Hire
Searles of Hunstanton, tel: 01485 534211; A E Wallis,

Heacham, tel: 01485 571683; Howletts Cycles, Dersingham, tel: 01483 543774; Great Bircham Mill, tel: 01485 578393

Nearest Railway Station
King's Lynn (16 miles/27km)

Refreshments
Many cafés and restaurants in

Cycle ride

SANDRINGHAM AND HUNSTANTON

Hunstanton and Heacham. En route are Great Bircham Mill tea room, Sandringham Country Park tea room/picnic areas and The Feathers, Dersingham. Wolferton Station Museum has toilets and a picnic area.

The seafront at Hunstanton

START

Hunstanton is a busy seaside resort on the A149 some 16 miles (26km) north of the ancient port and market town of King's Lynn. The town is well served with adequate on-street parking and designated car parks. If possible,

for the best position, park near The Green at the bottom of Greevegate. The route starts from the Town Hall which also houses the local Tourist Information Office.

SANDRINGHAM AND HUNSTANTON

Cycle ride

DIRECTIONS

1. Ride up Greevegate to the junction with the A149. Turn right, signposted 'Heacham', and after 500 yds (300m) pass the fire station and turn left into Downs Road, a gravelly track which improves. After ½ mile (1km) bear right and after another ½ mile (1km) bear left, keeping Downs Farm on your right. The lane crosses Ringstead Downs on a grassy surface.

2. On reaching a metalled road, turn right and cycle gently uphill to Sedgeford. If time permits turn right to visit the picturesque Heacham River and the round-towered church, whose graveyard gate commemorates a typhus epidemic of 1852. Otherwise turn left at the first junction and immediately right, on to the Fring Road. After about 2 miles (3km) Fring's All Saints Church will appear on the left, and then the village. At the junction, turn left and immediately right, past a dried-up village pond, towards Great Bircham. Before you reach the village, note the windmill on the right after about 2 miles (3km). Turn right into the lane leading to it.

3. The Mill stands beside a narrow lane. Continue along this lane and, at the next crossroads cross over on to a hard-surfaced lane and continue for 600 yds (549m) before bearing right and keeping on a similar track for 1 mile (1.5km). Come to a crossroads with the Peddars Way, an ancient track, now part of a long-distance path traversing north-west Norfolk; cross the Peddars Way, taking the left-hand fork, (this lane soon becomes tree-lined), and soon reach Anmer at an unusual Boy Scouts monument. Turn right, keeping the church on your left and, after the church turn second left on to a very narrow metalled lane. The brick water tower above West Newton soon comes into view; follow the road to the crossroads at West Newton.

4. Go straight over the crossroads, past the church, and take the first right into Sandringham Country Park. After visiting the park, follow the road to the next crossroads. For an optional loop via Wolferton (a good picnic spot), continue over the crossroads. Otherwise, turn right (see section 5) and continue for ½ mile (1km) flanked by silver birches to meet the A149. Go straight over, then turn left and downhill, past the old railway level-crossing cottage which retains its 'Beware of Trains' notice; follow the road round and back up to Wolferton Railway Museum. Continue uphill and soon fork left to reach the A149. Go straight across into Sandringham Country Park, past the folly on the left to a junction to re-join the route which omitted Wolferton.

5. Soon come to refreshment facilities and picnic areas on the left near Sandringham House. Continue for ½ mile (1km) and leave the park, turning left on to the B1440 soon to reach the village of Dersingham, with the Feathers Inn on the left and St Nicholas's Church on the right. Dersingham gave its name to Sandringham, as in the Domesday Book the manor was written as Sant-Dersingham. After the church bear left and then soon turn right up steep but short Fern Hill which becomes Mill Road. Soon turn left and continue to Ingoldisthorpe. Bear left at the junction, then right, keep the tree-surrounded church to your right. Cross Ingol stream and cycle uphill to the crossroads before Snettisham.

6. With Snettisham village and church on the left, go over the crossroads and bear right, then left to reach Sedgeford. At the junction turn left along the B1454 and continue to the A149, by the lavender distillery at Heacham. Go across on to Lynn Road and in 440 yds (402m) turn right on to Hunstanton Road, soon to reach the A149 which leads back to Hunstanton to complete the tour.

The beach at Hunstanton is long and sandy and ideal for games, walking and riding. North of the pier the sands are backed by the famous striped cliffs.

77

Cycle ride

SANDRINGHAM AND HUNSTANTON

The royal estate of Sandringham is well worth a visit

PLACES OF INTEREST

Hunstanton

This popular seaside town was founded as a resort in 1846. Its sandy beaches, shallow sea waters and striped cliffs – a geologist's dream – make it popular with holiday-makers of all ages. Children particularly enjoy the Oasis Leisure and Sealife Centres.

Ringstead Downs

Much of this area of mature woods and grassland with outcropping chalk is a Norfolk Naturalists Trust nature reserve, and its beech and ash trees are alive with woodland birds, as are the woods at Sandringham.

Great Bircham Mill

As the only windmill in the area open to the public, this is worth a visit. The mill comprises five floors, and visitors may also see the bakery, with its 200-year-old Peel oven, the tea rooms and gift shop, and the stables. The mill also offers cycle hire facilities, and has a play area for under 7s. Open Etr–Sep, daily.
Tel: 01485 578393

Sandringham

This famous estate was bought by Queen Victoria in 1862 for the future Edward VII. There is a huge parkland with woodland, picnic areas, restaurants, and gift shop. The museum and house grounds, and the house itself when the Royal family is not in residence, are open to the public.

Wolferton Station Museum

Once the Royal Station on the Sandringham Estate, this is set in a secluded wooded valley.

WHAT TO LOOK OUT FOR

Do not miss the striped cliffs of Hunstanton, the only hard rocky cliffs on the East Anglian coast, formed of white chalk over red chalk and carstone – a rust-brown sandstone. Look out for churches with round towers, nationally rare but common in East Anglia, as at Sedgeford. On Ringstead Downs in summer you should see stemless thistle, whilst great mullien and hoary mullien can be seen on roadside verges. The hawthorns, ash and beech trees on Ringstead Downs, and the extensive woodlands of Sandringham, are alive with birds, and a quiet wait with binoculars is sure to be rewarded.

SUTTON–SWAFFHAM

Sutton has the tallest windmill in Britain and the Broadlands Museum. Sutton Broad is a peaceful stretch of water frequented by birds, and is one of the main sources of reed used for thatching.

This charming market town, centred around Butter Cross in the main square, was once known as the 'Montpellier of England'. The market square is flanked with elegant 18th-century buildings. The northern end is dominated by the 1817 Assembly Rooms, while the Corn Exchange and Plowright Place are Victorian. Butter, or Market, Cross was presented to Swaffham by the Earl of Orford in 1783, and the handsome dome supported by pillars is topped by a statue of Ceres, the Roman goddess of agriculture. An open market, of ancient origin, is held here on Saturdays.

Swaffham's heyday was during the Regency period, where it was especially noted for its hare coursing. Wealthy farmers kept town houses here, for use in the winter. Swaffham was popular as a stop on the theatre circuit, and in 1806 the Nelsons and their party, including Lady Hamilton, attended a performance of *She Stoops to Conquer*.

The church was built of expensive Barnack stone, and tells of the wealth of medieval Swaffham. The north aisle owes its splendour to a poor peddler in the 15th century. The storey goes that John Chapman dreamt that he would meet a man who would make him rich in London. He set off, and met a man who told him that there was a pot of gold buried in his garden. He found two pots, and gave most of his new wealth to the church.

SUTTON
VILLAGE ON A149, 1 MILE (2KM) SE OF STALHAM

SWAFFHAM
TOWN OFF A47, 14 MILES (23KM) SE OF KING'S LYNN

The tallest mill in Britain at Sutton

gazetteer

THETFORD

THETFORD
TOWN ON A134, 12 MILES (19KM) N OF BURY ST EDMUNDS

THOMAS PAINE
1737–1809. English political writer. Constantly in trouble for his radical, revolutionary and anti-Christian opinions, Tom Paine came from Thetford, Norfolk (where there is a statue of him). In America from 1774, he wrote pamphlets in support of independence from England, and after his return home in 1787 he followed these by The Rights of Man *(1791–92), in praise of the French Revolution. He fled to Paris, was imprisoned for opposing the execution of Louis XVI and then returned to America.*

Ancient House Museum
WHITE HART ST
TEL: 01842 752599

Autumn colours in Thetford Forest

Pretty Thetford is associated with the atmospheric remains of a once-powerful abbey, a towering Norman castle mound set among Iron Age earthworks, and the great forest to the west. The town centre is a conservation area, so that the abundant medieval and Georgian houses in almost every street are protected.

Evidence of Thetford's early importance can be seen in its wealth of archaeological finds. There was a powerful Iron Age fortress here, which the practical Normans used as the base of their own castle in the 12th century. Perhaps even more important was the huge Cluniac priory that was founded by Roger Bigod, first Earl of Norfolk, in 1103, its picturesque ruins standing on the banks of the Little Ouse River.

In the town centre is the 15th-century Ancient House, now a museum. The fine carved oak ceilings can still be admired, and visitors can wander through the exhibitions on local history and archaeology. In the pretty courtyard is a Tudor herb garden. Near to the Ancient House is the birthplace of Thomas Paine, and there is a statue of him.

But perhaps best of Thetford's many treasures is the 50,000 acre (20,235 ha) Thetford Forest Park, great tracts of pine trees and heathland criss-crossed by ancient trackways.

An early Tudor timber-framed house with beautifully carved beamed ceilings, it now houses an exhibition on Thetford and Breckland life. This has been traced back to very early times, and there are examples from local Neolithic settlements. Brass rubbing facilities are available and there is a small period garden which has been

THETFORD

carefully recreated in the rear courtyard.
Open all year, most days. Closed Good Fri & Xmas period.

The Cluniac monastery was founded in 1103, and its remains are extensive. The 14th-century gatehouse of the priory stands to its full height, and the complete ground plan of the cloisters can be seen.
Open any reasonable time.

The remains of a two-storey hunting lodge, built in the 15th-century of flint with stone dressings.

Thetford Priory
(ON W SIDE OF THETFORD NEAR STATION)

Warren Lodge
2 MILES (3KM) W, ON B1107

Picnic site

THETFORD

LYNFORD STAG, THETFORD FOREST

Located east of the A134, Lynford Stag picnic site stands in the heart of the Thetford Forest Park, a vast area straddling Norfolk and Suffolk. Picnickers can enjoy the seclusion of one of the forest walks, of varying lengths, or stay in the attractive picnic area, where there is an excellent children's playground.

HOW TO GET THERE
The site is well signposted off the A134 and at the entrance. It lies about 1½ miles (2.5km) south-east of Mundford.

FACILITIES
A 60-acre (24-ha) flat, grassy area surrounded by trees, with plenty of picnic tables scattered around.

Parking for about 200 cars in several different areas, including one for disabled people.

Toilets, noticeboards containing information about local forest events, and children's play area.

Three easy, waymarked, colour-coded walks through the forest, ranging from 1¼ miles (2km) to 2½ miles (4km) in length.

A secluded forest walk

THETFORD

𝒫icnic site

LYNFORD STAG, THETFORD FOREST

In the 1930s, Forestry Commission workers made a curious discovery. In a clearing stood a full-sized model of a stag, made of iron complete with metal antlers. The stag had been made by a landowner called Sir Richard Sutton, reputed to be an excellent shot, who used it for target practice between 1824 and 1855. The forest clearing is now the picnic site, which is named after the metal stag, with the 19th-century ruins of Lynford Hall standing in the forest near by. Picnic tables are set among pine, chestnut, and beech trees, while grassy tracks lead off into the forest to provide marked trails, including the 24-mile (38.5-km) walk to West Stow which passes through the picnic site.

Thetford Priory

THETFORD FOREST

Spanning two counties, Thetford Forest is a 50,000-acre (20,235-ha) area of lowland pine forest and heathland owned by the Forestry Commission. Planting was started in 1922, and the woodland growth has attracted many birds and animals – there are four species of deer, and the rare red squirrel thrives here.

Thetford was the site of a series of Danish raids in the 9th and 11th centuries. By 1012, the Danes had control over most of East Anglia, and their king, Sweyne, made Thetford his capital. His successor Cnut also used Thetford as his capital. It became even more important after the Norman conquest when Arfast established a new bishopric here.

CLOSE BY

Grimes Graves, a 4,000-year-old Neolithic flint mine owned by English Heritage and open all year, lies 1 mile (1.5km) to the south. The fascinating tunnels and pits were first discovered in the 1970s, and visitors can descend a ladder into one of them. To the south-east by five miles (8km) is the market town of Thetford. The entire town centre is a conservation area, and Thetford also boasts a priory with a 14th-century gatehouse (owned by English Heritage; open all year), and a massive castle mound.
(See also page 85.)

THURSFORD—WALPOLE, ST ANDREW & ST PETER

THURSFORD COLLECTION
TEL: *01328 878477*
AT THURSFORD, HAMLET OFF
A148, 5 MILES (8KM) NE OF
FAKENHAM

This exciting collection specialises in organs, with a Wurlizter cinema organ, fairground organs, barrel organs and street organs among its treasures. There are live musical shows every day, featuring all the material organs and the Wurlitzer show. The collection also includes showmen's engines, ploughing engines and farm machinery. There is a children's play area and a breathtaking 'Venetian gondola' switchback ride. Special evening musical events, details on request, and various shops with a Dickensian touch.

Open Apr–Oct, daily.

TITCHWELL RSPB NATURE RESERVE
TEL: *01485 210432*
HAMLET ON A149, 6 MILES
(9.5KM) E OF HUNSTANTON

This is one of the RSPB's most popular coastal reserves at all times of the year be it for summer avocets or wintering waders and wildfowl. A firm path takes you to three hides and on to the beach where a platform overlooking the sea is suitable for wheelchairs. A colony of avocets nest on the enclosed marsh with gadwalls, tufted ducks, shovelers and blackheaded gulls. Bearded tits, water rails, bitterns and marsh harriers are found on the reedbeds. Common and little terns, ringed plovers and oystercatchers nest on the beach where large flocks of waders roost during the highest autumn tides. Many migrants visit the marsh including wigeon, black-tailed godwits, curlews, sandpipers and occasional rarities. In winter, brent geese and goldeneyes occur regularly with divers, grebes and seaducks offshore and snow bunting foraging on the beach. Phone for details of special events.

Open at all times. Visitor Centre daily.

TRIMINGHAM
VILLAGE ON B1159, 4 MILES
(6KM) SE OF CROMER

A North Norfolk coastal village with a church dedicated to the Head of John the Baptist. There is plenty of exquisite woodcarving by a former rector.

UPTON
VILLAGE OFF B1140, 2 MILES
(3KM) N OF ACLE

A medium-sized village, Upton stands near a marshy stretch of land locally called The Doles, near Upton Broad. St Margaret's church, built in the Perpendicular style, lies to the south of the village. At its eastern edge, near the end of (1km) Upton Dyke, stands the Palmers Hollow Post Mill, the only drainage windpump on the Broads with a plunger pump.

WALPOLE, ST ANDREW AND ST PETER
VILLAGES OFF A47, 6 MILES
(10KM) NE OF WISBECH

In 1216 King John lost his treasure as his retinue passed through the parish of Walpole St Andrew. Searches for this fabled wealth continue today. Walpole St Peter boasts one of the finest churches in the Norfolk marshlands. The family of Hugh Walpole, Britain's first Prime Minister, left Walpole in the 13th century.

WEETING

Grimes Graves

The parish of Weeting contains Grimes Graves and the ruins of a castle.

The neolithic flint mines at Grimes Graves round barrows close by, are open to visit. Some Iron-Age pottery and Roman pottery has been found locally.
(See also Picnic: Lynford Stag, Thetford Forest, page 82.)

This ruined 11th-century fortified manor house is situated in a rectangular moated enclosure. It is interesting for its slight remains of a three-storeyed cross-wing, and ice-house built by William Warrenne.
Open any reasonable time.

WEETING
VILLAGE ON B1106, 2 MILES (3KM) N OF BRANDON

Grimes Graves

Weeting Castle

WELLS-NEXT-THE-SEA—WELNEY

Wells-Next-The-Sea

WELLS-NEXT-THE-SEA
SMALL TOWN ON A149, 6
MILES (10KM) E OF BURNHAM
MARKET

A working harbour town with a quayside filled with colourful boats and dock equipment. No longer by the sea, Wells stands on a muddy creek. The Embankment, a mile long, was built to prevent the harbour from silting up altogether, and provides a pleasant walk to the sea. A local delicacy, pickled samphire, can be bought here.

**WELLS & WALSINGHAM
LIGHT RAILWAY**
TEL: 01328 856506
(TIMETABLE)
(WELLS STATION, SHERINGHAM
RD (A149). WALSINGHAM
STATION, EGMERE RD).

The railway covers the 4 miles (6.5km) between Wells and Walsingham. It is unusual in that it uses 10¼-in gauge track and is the longest track of this gauge in the world. The line passes through some very attractive countryside, particularly noted for its wild flowers and butterflies. This is the home of the unique Garratt steam locomotive specially built for this line.

WELNEY
VILLAGE ON A1101, 5 MILES
(8KM) NW OF LITTLEPORT

A small village sited on the Ouse Washes, famous as the home of Welney Washes Nature Reserve.

WWT Welney
PINTAIL HOUSE, HUNDRED FOOT
BANK
TEL: 01353 860711

This internationally important wetland site on the beautiful Ouse Washes is famed for the breathtaking spectacle of wild ducks, geese and swans which spend the winter there. Impressive observation facilities, including hides, towers and an observatory, offer outstanding views of the huge numbers of wildfowl which include Bewick's and whooper swans, wigeon, teal and shoveler. During summer, a nature walk across the reserve, through rich carpets of yellow, pink and purple wildflowers, looking for waders and warblers, is a delightful experience. Other features include floodlit evening swan feeds

WEST RUNTON–WEYBOURNE

between November and February, an exhibition area, gift shop and tea room. Facilities for disabled people include access to the main observatory, two hides for wheelchair users and access along 1 mile (1.5km) of the summer nature walk.

Open all year, daily. Closed 25 Dec.

The beach is safe for swimming, and was once a source of amber. Runton Church is ancient, with a 13th-century tower and a dozen carved poppy heads.

WEST RUNTON
VILLAGE ON A149, 2 MILES (3KM) E OF SHERINGHAM

The Shire Horse Centre has a collection of draught horses and nine breeds of mountain and moorland ponies. There are also exhibits of horse-drawn machinery, waggons and carts, and harnessing and working demonstrations are given twice every day. Other attractions include a children's farm, a photographic display of draught horses past and present, talks and a video show. There is a riding school on the premises as well.

Open late Mar–late Oct, most days. Shire horse demonstrations mornings and afternoons.

Norfolk Shire Horse Centre
WEST RUNTON STABLES
TEL: 01263 837339

A pleasing little village near Martham Broad and the River Thurne. 'Norfolk giant' Robert Hales was born here. He was almost 8ft (2m) tall.

WEST SOMERTON
VILLAGE ON B1159, 2 MILES (3KM) W OF WINTERTON-ON-SEA

The steep shingle beach is called Weybourne Hoop (or Hope). It was considered a vulnerable spot during the Armada crisis and in both world wars.

WEYBOURNE
VILLAGE ON A149, 3 MILES (5KM) W OF SHERINGHAM

The Muckleburgh Collection is the largest privately-owned military collection of its kind in the UK and incorporates the Museum of the Suffolk and Norfolk Yeomanry dating from the 18th century. Its 3,000 exhibits include restored and working tanks, armoured cars, trucks and artillery of World War II, and equipment including weapons from the Falklands and the Gulf War. Special model displays and diorama include military vehicles, aircraft and ships as well as radios and uniforms. Live tank demonstrations are run daily during summer high season. New exhibits include a Harrier GR3, a 155 Howitzer brought back from the Falkland Islands, a room dedicated to the role of the Royal Air Force in East Anglia, a Scorpion AFV and a Rapier field standard B1(m) fire unit – the only one of its kind on display across the world.

Open Feb–Oct, daily.

The Muckleburgh Collection
WEYBOURNE MILITARY CAMP
TEL: 01263 588210 & 588608

WOODBASTWICK—WYMONDHAM

WOODBASTWICK
VILLAGE OFF A1151, 8 MILES (12KM) NE OF NORWICH

This is probably the most attractive village in the Broads, with thatched houses and a round thatched pumphouse set around a neat green. Cockshoot Broad nearby was restored by the Broads Authority in 1982 to clear water. A nature trail now runs along Cockshoot Dyke.

WROXHAM
VILLAGE ON A1151, 7 MILES (11KM) NE OF NORWICH

Linked to Hoveton by an attractive hump-backed bridge, Wroxham is generally acknowledged to be the capital of the Norfolk Broads. It was here in the late 1800s that the now thriving boat-hire industry began. The river banks are jammed tightly with boats of all sizes and colours. Further on is the unnavigable Hoveton Great Broad with its nature trail.

WYMONDHAM
SMALL TOWN ON A11, 9 MILES (14KM) SW OF NORWICH

At the centre of this charming market town (pronounced 'Windham') is its handsome octagonal market cross. This was built of wood in 1617. Also long surviving is the Guild Chapel dedicated to Thomas á Becket and rebuilt in the 14th century; it is now home to the County Library.

The splendid abbey church of St Mary and St Thomas of Canterbury has two towers due to a 14th-century dispute between the monks and the townspeople. In the 13th century, the Benedictine monks of the priory here quarelled so badly with the people that the Pope gave the nave, north-west tower and the north aisle to the people, and the remainder to the monks. After the people built the present Great West Tower in 1445, the monks erected their own octagonal one.

By the Bure at Wroxham

88

WINTERTON

Walk

A pleasant walk through dunes and farmland that shows a flat landscape is not necessarily a dull one.

THE DUNES AT WINTERTON

Grid ref: TG498197

INFORMATION

The walk is 5½ miles (9km) long. Mostly level ground, though dune walking can be harder.
Groynes to negotiate on the shoreline.
Some road walking on a quiet lane.
Café at car park in summer.
Pub in Winterton.
Toilets in the village.
The sandy beach is ideal for picnics.

START

Winterton lies about 8 miles (13km) north of Great Yarmouth, on the B1159. Start the walk from the beach car park at the eastern end of the village – a charge is made in summer.

DIRECTIONS

Walk back towards the village and turn right before the first bungalow. Continue across the sand hills and turn left on to a track between two houses. Go straight ahead at the crossroads and continue on this track towards East Somerton for about ¾ mile (1km), passing Winterton church and farm buildings on the left. The track bends right past Manor Farm and a ruined church, and bear right on the concrete track beyond Burnley Hall. At the next junction bear left, and turn right just before the trees. Continue on this roadway for about ½ mile (1km), and turn right on a rough track.

After a short distance, turn left, keeping the hedge on your left, towards some farm buildings. Turn right here, keeping the buildings to your left, and follow the track towards the sea, reaching a gate on your right beyond some trees. (For a slightly longer walk, go straight ahead here to cross the dunes, walking back to the car park along the shoreline). Pass through the gate, and follow the track along the back of the sand hills for just over 1 mile (1.5km), back to Winterton. Follow the track between two houses, and at the crossroads turn left to retrace your route back to the car park.

A storm-wracked coastline

Often appearing deceptively peaceful, this stretch of coast was notorious for its shipwrecks in stormy weather. The 18th-century writer Daniel Defoe reported that half the village of Winterton was built of timbers from wrecked vessels, and in one winter's night 200 coal ships were lost offshore. Tombstones in the church bear witness to the many lives lost.

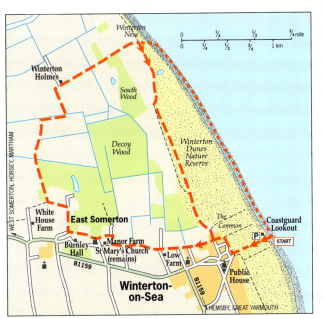

89

Walk

WINTERTON

WINTERTON

The tall tower of Winterton church serves as a good landmark

The sea has also invaded this coastline, breaking through the dunes and flooding the land. Since the most recent flooding, in 1938, the dunes have been reinforced with concrete in some places.

 WHAT TO LOOK OUT FOR

The dune system is a National Nature Reserve, and rich in a variety of wildlife. The drier areas of the dunes support heather, and ferns and other wetland plants grow on damper patches. Watch out for adders. Little terns nest on the beach, so keep to the main track and observe all warning signs to avoid disturbing them.

LISTINGS

ACTIVITIES

Angling

With the Broads, rivers, small lakes for freshwater fish and the coast for sea-angling, you are never far away from excellent fishing in Norfolk. General information is available from the Environment Agency (previously the National Rivers Authority), see Useful Addresses and Numbers, page 92.

Beaches

There are some wonderful sandy beaches in Norfolk, and some that are shingle. On the North Norfolk coast, there are wide beaches where the tide goes out for miles; on the east coast, they tend to be narrower and shelve steeply. When bathing, remember that the current flows south on the flood and north on the ebb and can run quite strongly, especially when the wind is in the same direction. There are sometimes onshore easterly winds, so a windbreak can be useful.

Birdwatching

The varied coast from the Wash, along the soft cliffs down to the sand and shingle beaches, provides excellent viewing. The best visiting seasons are given where applicable.

Cley Marshes (Norfolk Wildlife Trust)
5 miles (8km) NW of Holt
Coastal wetland. Waders, wildfowl, rarities, bittern, bearded tit. The variety of habitats make it an unusual site. The reserve has saltwater and freshwater marsh, reed-bed and grazing marsh. Access at all times on footpaths, beach and roads; most hides always open. Open all year (closed Mondays except bank holidays). Visitor centre open April to October, 10am to 5pm. Tel: 01263 740008.

Ranworth Broad (Norfolk Wildlife Trust)
4 miles (6km) NW of Acle
Woodland, reed-bed. Situated in the middle section of the River Bure. Common terns, swallows, teal wideon, shoveler, pochard, gadwall, cormorant. Open all year. Ranworth conservation centre open April to October, 10am to 5pm. Tel: 01603 270479.

Snettisham Bird Reserve (RSPB)
near King's Lynn, just off A149
Coastal wetland. Waders, wildfowl. Open at all times. Best visited in spring, autumn, winter, at or around high tide. Tel: 01485 542689.

Strumpshaw Fen (RSPB)
near Brundall, E of Norwich
Grazing marsh, fen. Fen flowers, marsh harrier, Cetti's warbler. Open 9am to 9pm or dusk, whichever is earlier. Best visited in spring, early summer.

Titchwell Marsh (RSPB)
5 miles (8km) E of Hunstanton
Coastal wetland. Marsh harrier, waders, rarities, little tern, wildfowl.

Welney Wildfowl Refuge (Wildfowl Trust)
5 miles (8km) NW of Littleport
Wetland. Bewick's and whooper swans, wigeon, pintail. Permit from Wildfowl Trust, fee to non-WT members. The classic time to visit is winter, but a summer trail is also open.

USEFUL ADDRESSES AND NUMBERS

Broads Authority, Thomas Harvey House,
18 Colegate, Norwich
Tel: 01603 610734

English Heritage (EH),
The Area Manager, Castle Acre Priory,
Castle Acre
Tel: 01760 755161

Environment Agency, Kingfisher House,
Peterborough, Cambridgeshire
Tel: 01480 414581

National Trust (NT), The Regional Director ,
Blickling Hall, Blickling

Tel: 01263 733471

Norfolk and Suffolk Yachting Association
The Secretary, 46 Teresa Road, Stalham
Tel: 01692 581124

Norfolk Museums Service ,
Castle Museum, Norwich
Tel: 01603 223624

Royal Society for the Protection of Birds (RSPB),
Stalham House, 65 Thorpe Road, Norwich
Tel: 01603 661662

TOURIST INFORMATION CENTRES

Attleborough, Victoria Gallery, Cypress House,
Queen Square
Tel: 01953 452404

Aylsham*, Bure Valley Railway Station,
Norwich Road
Tel: 01263 733903

Cromer, The Bus Station, Prince of Wales Road
Tel: 01263 512497

Dereham*, The Bell Tower, St Nicholas
Church
Tel: 01362 698992

Diss, Meresmouth, Mere Street,
Tel: 01379 650523

Downham Market, Town Hall, Bridge Street
Tel: 01366 387440

Fakenham*, Red Lion House, Market Place
Tel: 01328 851981

Great Yarmouth, Town Hall
Tel: 01493 846345

Marine Parade*
Tel: 01493 842195

North West Tower*, Quay
Tel: 01493 332095

Holt, Market Place
Tel: 01263 713100

LISTINGS

Hoveton*, Station Road
Tel: 01603 782281

Hunstanton, The Green
Tel: 01485 532610

King's Lynn, The Old Gaol House, Saturday
Market Place
Tel: 01553 763044

Loddon*,41 Bridge Street,
Tel: 01508 520690

Mundesley*, 2A Station Road
Tel: 01263 721070

North Walsham*, Brentnal House,
32 Vicarage Street
Tel: 01692 407509

Norwich, The Guildhall, Gaol Hill
Tel: 01603 666071

Ranworth*, The Staithe
Tel: 01603 270453

Sheringham*, Station Approach
Tel: 01263 824329

Swaffham*, Market Place
Tel: 01760 722255

Thetford, Ancient House Museum, White
Hart Street
Tel: 01842 752599

Walsingham*, Shirehall Museum,
Common Place
Tel: 01328 820510

Watton*, The Clock Tower, High Street
Tel: 01953 882058

Wells-next-the-Sea*, Staithe Street
Tel: 01328 710885

Wymondham*, Market Cross, Market Place
Tel: 01953 604721

* Denotes seasonal opening only

INDEX

Acle 6
Attleborough 6
Aylsham 6, 7
Baconsthorpe Castle 6
Banham Zoo 6
Binham 6
Blickling Hall 7–10
Breckland 37
Bressingham 11
Broads, The 12–19
Brundall 20
Bure Valley Railway 20–1
Burgh Castle 22
Burnham Market 22, 49–52
Burnham Norton 22
Burnham Overy 22
Burnham Thorpe 22–4, 49–52
Caister-on-Sea 25
Caister St Edmund 25
Castle Acre 27–8
Castle Rising 25–6
Cawston 29
Cley Marshes/Blakeney Point 32–3
Cley-Next-The-Sea 29–31
Cockley Cley 34
Coltishall 34
Cromer 34–5
Diss 35
Downham Market 35
East Dereham 35
East Harling 36–7
Eccles 38
Erpingham 38
Fakenham 39, 72
Felbrigg 39
Filby 40
Fleggburgh, The Village 40
Fritton 40
Geldeston 40

Glandford 40
Gooderstone 40
Great Bircham 78
Great Witchingham 40–1
Great Yarmouth 42–5
Gressenhall 41
Grimes Graves 83, 85
Heacham 46
Heydon 10, 46
Hickling 46
Hindringham 46
Hingham 46
Holkham Hall/Park 49–52
Holme Next The Sea 46–7
Holt 47
Horning 47
Horsey 48
Horsham St Faith 48
Horstead 48
Houghton Hall 53
Hunstanton 75–8
King's Lynn 53–4
Langham 54
Langley Green 54
Letheringsett 55
Little Dunham 55
Little Walsingham 52, 55–6,
Loddon 56
Long Stratton 56
Ludham Marshes 57–8
Lynford Stag 82–3
Mannington Hall Gardens 10, 59,
Marriott Way, The 7–10
Martham 59
Mundesley 60
Neatishead 60
North Creake 52
North Norfolk Railway 61–2
North Walsham 60

Norwich 63–70
Oxburgh Hall 71
Paston 72
Pensthorpe 72
Ranworth 72
Reedham 72
Reepham 73
Ringstead Downs 78
St Olave's Priory 73
Salle 10
Sandringham 75–8
Scole 73
Sheringham 73
Shipdham 73
Snettisham 73
South Walsham 74
Stalham 74
Stow Bardolph 74
Strumpshaw 74
Sutton 79

Swaffham 79
Thetford/Thetford Forest 80–3
Thursford Collection 84
Titchwell RSPB Nature Reserve 84
Trimingham 84
Upton 84
Walpole, St Andrew and St Peter 84
Weeting 85
Wells & Walsingham Light Railway 86
Wells-Next-The-Sea 86
Welney 86–7
West Runton 87
West Somerton 87
Weybourne 87
Winterton 89–90
Wolferton 78
Woodbastwick 88
Wroxham 88
Wymondham 88

ACKNOWLEDGEMENTS

The Automobile Association wishes to thank the following photographers for their assistance in the preparation of this book.

A Baker 16, 18/9, 30/1, 34, 55, 62/3, 68/9, 78, 79, 80/1, 85; M Birkett 7, 8, 9,10, 20/1, 48, 49, 50, 51, 82; P Davies 86; A Edwards 36; R J Elliott 26, 60/1; D Forss 28, 58, 90; A Hopkins 32; S&O Matthews 14, 29, 38, 39, 52, 71, 75, 76, 83; A Perkins 42/3, 45, 47; T Souter 9, 13, 33, 53, 88; A Tryner 27; L Whitwam 64/5, 66/7; H Williams 41; T Woodcock 6, 11.

Cover photographs
INTERNATIONAL PHOTOBANK front – main
STEVE WATKINS/NATURAL EXPOSURE – front cover cyclists
A Baker: back – top
L Whitwam: back.– middle
WORLD PICTURES back – bottom

Trouble MAKER

NEW YORK TIMES BESTSELLING AUTHOR
DEBORAH
BLADON